D1300349

SCULPTURE AT GOODWOOD

www.sculpture.org.uk

British Contemporary Sculpture at Goodwood 1997-98

As knowledge of Sculpture at Goodwood spreads internationally, we have been delighted to see that collectors and curators appreciate the work here, and have acquired good pieces. Equally, we have noted that many who wish to commission sculptures for a particular site use Sculpture at Goodwood as an example to test their ideas and to consider how an artist's work may be seen on a large scale, which is not normally possible in a gallery or studio space. These factors, and the enthusiam of our visitors, have enabled us to plan with confidence for the long-term future.

Sculpture at Goodwood's collection of sculptors' drawings has grown immeasurably this year. The quality and originality of the drawings which artists donate when a sculpture is commissioned is impressive. Some of these are illustrated in this book, and an exhibition of Sculpture at Goodwood Drawings which will travel abroad will be launched in 1998. We are delighted that sculptors have made this initiative possible, and thank them warmly for their generosity.

The sequence of sculptures in this book reflects the order in which visitors are likely to view them.

We are grateful, as ever, for those who have helped us throughout the year, and whose names are listed at the end of the book. In particular we should like to single out for our very special thanks Dr Christopher Thorpe who has worked tirelessly to create the Sculpture at Goodwood Website, and Professor Norbert Lynton who has written especially for this, our third volume.

Wilfred and Jeannette Cass

Making Seen the Unseen

The gates leading into Sculpture at Goodwood are set into a noble wall, high and appearing infinitely long, built of Sussex flints and mortar by prisoners of war taken out of Napoleon's army. Two sculptures greet visitors outside those gates. On the left is Sir Anthony Caro's *Goodwood Steps*, an indoor sculpture made and shown in Halifax, now drastically reshaped by the artist at Goodwood for its out-of-doors location. His words about that can be found on page 14 of this book. On the right stands Ana Maria Pacheco's *Requiem*, a poetic work dominated by a stone figure of a man in bathing trunks, at once mighty and pathetic; the account on page 16 tells of how it was carved at Goodwood.

My comments on Sculpture at Goodwood begin with these two sculptures and where they stand in order to draw attention to key aspects of the collection. The first of these relates to time, to chronology. The collection presents contemporary British sculpture, and this means not just work by living artists but work done recently. When the site opened, in September 1994, the net was cast more widely; now it brings in new work only. Many of the artists involved have world-wide reputations; all are well established. So what is on show is fresh and innovatory work by substantial artists.

The second relates to style and idiom. We call the Caro abstract, the Pacheco figurative. The collection is about quality as well as newness, but it is not guided by preconceptions derived from theoretical categories, let alone any prejudice regarding materials. Wilfred and Jeannette Cass and Ann Elliott, Head of Sculpture, agree that finding and choosing the right pieces is not difficult: interesting new work emerges constantly and it is pretty clear what will do well at Goodwood. No prejudices operate. To some, the Caro steel construction and the Pacheco stone and multi media enactment might seem contradictory, works of art from opposite sides of dispute. Here we discover that they address each other. The Pacheco speaks of death as a release from wordly burdens; the Caro *Steps* have taken on a new significance by lifting our eyes up to the sweeping Sussex skies. The latter floats just above the ground, a mighty band of steel curved and folded to become a man-made mountain range in form, a resounding fugal passage from a great organ in expression, raising our spirits above this earth. Both these modern works have deep connections throughout human history, to pyramids and ziggurats, to gigantic temples and temple figures, to stage sets and mystery plays, devotional figures and marionettes. This surely is one of the central achievements of modern art that, in rejecting one exclusive academic tradition, it has given us, and continues to give us, access to a much wider world of signification through creative work. It takes an open-minded gathering such as is offered here to make us aware of that.

The third relates to time again, to change. Neither of these sculptures will be here for very long. One of them may well have gone before readers of these words reach the gates. Others will take their places; other confrontations will yield other thoughts. It is not a conscious aim of Sculpture at Goodwood to stimulate ideas about art and humanity, but it is a primary concern to place sculpture to its best advantage, so that its form and material, its surface qualities and its scale, are given fullest expression. To this end - and in this it is surely unique - this is not a permanent static colllection. It does not accumulate; it does not rest on its laurels; it constantly renews itself. At present about a third of the works exhibited will be replaced each year. When the Pacheco goes the Caro will become a slightly different work, offering a somewhat different experience. When that goes the location itself, outside the gates, will take on a different character. There is no predicting how exactly, even whether, these sites will be used another time.

Nor - fourth point - is it a conveyor belt for sculpture borrowed here and there for temporary display. A growing proportion of the exhibits each year is commissioned or facilitated by Sculpture at Goodwood. That is, sculptors are invited to make a piece for Goodwood - it is sometimes their first opportunity to make work for the kind of position and scale offered here - or they are enabled to give exhibitable form to a project that already exists as a maquette and/or in impermanent materials. Full-scale casts and constructions or very large carvings are often beyond the purses of individual artists, as are the transporting, lifting and placing, the preparation of the ground to suit each piece. These are in the care of Goodwood: the outlay, the skill and the experience. When a piece sells, what money is gained after the artist and the dealer or agent have received their share, is ploughed back into further commissions and other costs. This point, in conjunction with those concerned with newness and with an open-ended view of what modern sculpture can be, guarantees a display that is at once purposeful and productive but also developmental and self-challenging. At every visit there is something new to engage with, and each visiting sculpture affects the complexion of the whole.

The grounds themselves change too. Hat Hill Copse is in a designated Area of Outstanding Natural Beauty. Changes are wrought by Nature herself as the seasons and the years pass. Just now, bluebells are beginning to show beneath the tall trees. The land slopes gently to the south and offers open areas and ancient woodland, winding paths from glade to glade, and far views along grassy avenues, over low fields and meadows to Chichester and the sea. It feels infinite. The layout invites us to wander from sculpture to sculpture, guided by a leaflet that has to be updated constantly. Much of the work done to the grounds relates to the coming and going of the exhibits. Sites have to be prepared and later made good. But the grounds have also been undergoing a delicate programme of cleaning and tidying, of removing excessive undergrowth, letting in air and light and enabling wild flowers to grow again where they had been smothered. The touch is light: nature and some controlling of nature go hand in hand in a way that feels essentially English. The thought arises that the principle we associate with Post-Impressionism and its heritage - that art springs from a collaboration with materials and processes, not from overcoming them and denying their character - has its origins in the English tradition of landscape gardening as well as, more obviously, in radical developments in British design and the applied arts, in and after the later nineteenth century.

It follows quite naturally that Sculpture at Goodwood has taken an interest in contemporary British design as a contributing factor to the site, useful, pleasing and innovative. This interest goes back to Tom Heatherwick's acrylic, wood and aluminium *Pavilion* the Casses set up in 1991. It has been furthered in the various seats, from *Garden Throne* to *Kissing Seat*, that have been added since. The design programme has a fitting climax in Craig Downie's *Gallery and Reception* building, built in 1994, and in its furniture. New design items are added every year.

In the first of its books, published in 1995, the aims of the charitable foundation that runs Sculpture at Goodwood were summarised as 'to promote the understanding, enjoyment and development of contemporary sculpture through education and support for sculptors and designers, and to act as both a focus and a catalyst for siting contemporary sculpture in the open air'. All this demands close contact with sculptural activity in the country, with the broad scene and with individual artists. The artists are closely involved with the translation of their work and its siting at Goodwood. In many instances, they make their work at Goodwood and can be seen doing so. The underlying theme of collaboration is thus restated: artists and their materials, Goodwood and the artists, the works themselves and the natural setting they are afforded here. This, in addition to the financial and practical help given to sculptors, is a major contribution to the development of contemporary sculpture.

'Understanding and enjoyment' call for something additional. From the start, all at Goodwood have seen it as essential to provide information about the sculpture in a variety of forms. These range from issuing printed information and records, to providing trained volunteer guides for visitors, to the fast developing exploitation of electronic media from compact discs on the work of individual artists, to constantly updated website information. The series of events called 'Sculpture on Saturdays' has been of great value, bringing sculptors to Goodwood to speak about their work in general and about the piece on exhibition, and to be questioned about it by an art critic and by the audience. The media associate new art with shock and aversion. These sessions prove again and again the creative seriousness as well as the intelligence of artists, and also how difficulties melt away when attention instead of quick rejection is offered.

Clearly, Sculpture at Goodwood cannot accommodate everything. The concept 'sculpture' has widened extraordinarily in modern times. Ephemeral work such as Happenings and Performance Art cannot be installed; almost all installation sculpture calls for a built space. Much Conceptual Art is immaterial and transitory and depends on that indeterminacy. Yet the range of what Goodwood presents has grown. Risks are considered and taken, from Andy Goldsworthy's reconstructing, half hidden along the trees, his Dumfrieshire dry-stone arches, to having Vong Phaophanit's electronic *Azure Neon Body* glow mysteriously out of its trench in the ground. Smaller sculptures can be installed in the Gallery and Reception pavilion. There will always be limits to what Goodwood can do, but they are constantly in question.

Skilful siting plays a major role in all this. Placing sculpture out of doors has a long history, but not all sculpture shows up well in the open air, and some kinds of sculpture will do better in urban spaces than in natural settings. Of these Goodwood offers a great variety; long vistas, secluded glades with open skies, places under trees that can make sculpture seem either part of nature or a mysterious, alien visitor , sunken areas or raised platforms that can embrace or proffer sculpture in distinct ways. Different forms and materials call for differing degrees and kinds of visibility. Thus Sculpture at Goodwood is building a body of experience from which all the world can benefit, while providing a broad, cumulative view of one of the most remarkable streams of artistic invention and production in the world. Its fame, which is also the fame of the artists involved and of British sculpture in general, is global.

Norbert Lynton

The title for Professor Lynton's essay is taken from *Hat Hill Copse*, a poem by Dr Christopher Fry, printed in *Sculpture at Goodwood 95/96*.

A Different Mould

Some people have expressed feelings of puzzlement about Sculpture at Goodwood, wondering why it is different from other venues which show sculpture in the open air. They want to know how it works and the reasons for its difference. Since we are now three years into developing the Foundation, and have found the structure to work very well indeed, it would seem the right moment to restate the basic aims and philosophy. This is the only venue in Britain where visitors can see an extensive range of work by major and emerging British sculptors, all of which has been enabled by Sculpture at Goodwood. Over a three-year period most of the sculptures change as more work is commissioned, replacing those pieces that have been sold; a process which has been devised to ensure diversity and to encourage the purchase of contemporary British sculpture.

Everyone associated with Sculpture at Goodwood holds a stake in the organisation, even though this fact is not formally acknowledged. The artists, their galleries and agents, the founders, trustees, staff, visitors and volunteers, all contribute towards making the venue viable, and help to support and promote the sculpture of our time. When Wilfred Cass devised the business plan for the enterprise, he saw his financial and philosophical investment as a contribution parallel to the effort of others. Central to his vision is the contribution of the sculptors. Their ideas for sculpture always come first, followed by the Foundation's financial support in realising the work, showing it to great advantage and promoting the pieces through Sculpture at Goodwood books, the Internet, the media and Sculpture on Saturday study days.

Visitors to Sculpture at Goodwood pay an entrance fee for every visit. We see this, not as a toll, but as their contribution to making the venue work, for themselves, their fellow visitors and for the artists. Visitors are also paying for the changing of works, much as visitors to the special exhibitions in art galleries and museums pay for each new show.

A team of some thirty volunteers give their time freely to Sculpture at Goodwood. The guides' stake is to make visitors welcome, to provide information about the sculptures and the Foundation. They are a vital resource, and enrich the venue with their commitment and enthusiasm. Of equal importance are those who work behind the scenes, the volunteer technicians, accountants from KPMG, computer and Website consultants, forestry and garden designers, all of whom contribute their specialist and professional skills. The continuing support and encouragement of the Duke of Richmond and Goodwood Estate staff have enabled Sculpture at Goodwood to grow and to explore ways of promoting the venue that are innovative and would not otherwise be possible. Image Bank, the photographic stills and film library run by Mark Cass, supports the Foundation and is helping to explore new ways of perceiving sculpture by means of new technology and virtual reality.

A frequent query is how artists are selected to show their work at Sculpture at Goodwood. The work of British sculptors is a vital force internationally. Its diversity and scale led to the pragmatic decision that here was plenty with which to operate, and confirmed the founders' choice of working only with British artists. Wilfred and Jeannette Cass, together with their curator, keep a very close eye on current sculptural practice. Decisions about the artists whose work is to be commissioned are made with particular regard for timing. Supporting an artist may be appropriate at a certain period, when a change of direction or new development can be fostered. We find that Goodwood's intervention becomes a catalyst, either consolidating a series of work or generating new exploration.

The landscape at Sculpture at Goodwood is continually modified to accommodate new sculptures and to improve the environment.

Sculptures are seen as individual pieces, with no artfully created links with other work, and everything that is done to the landscape is also done in this spirit. So far most of the works exhibited rest on the assumption that the object is paramount. The fact that other modes of expression have not yet been addressed should not be seen as a mission to exclude them. Sound, water, the moving image are all possibilities, provided that the constraints of an outdoor venue can be employed in a way that such pieces may be seen well.

Educational projects have evolved as information technology has been harnessed to the needs of Sculpture at Goodwood. Early experiments with interactive systems proved to be too cumbersome, and recent headway through use of the Internet has endorsed plans to exploit its possibilities more fully. The Sculpture at Goodwood Website, designed by Dr Christopher Thorpe of [overwired...], at the time of press, occupies some four hundred pages which are devoted to an archive of all the sculptures that have been shown here, texts, photographs and artists' biographies, pages of background information, sound and video and a virtual tour. Current information in Sculpture of the Month outlines the changes which take place and introduces potential visitors to new items. The educational value of the site is exploited to enable visitors and researchers to plan their visits in considerable detail. Students also find it easy to prepare fully in order to get the most from their visits. Gradually, artists' working methods and the industrial processes of fabrication and casting are being recorded in relation to the sculptures commissioned, and are being added to the Website. Broadcasts in the form of stills and videos of artists working on site have already been placed in the archive to build what is hoped will be a major resource in the years to come. Sculpture on Saturday study days are recorded and broadcast on the day they take place.

Looking to the future, Sculpture at Goodwood will continue to commission around twelve sculptures a year, with the unknown aspects of this adventure lying in the fertile imagination of present and future British sculptors.

Ann Elliott, Head of Sculpture

Sir Anthony Caro
Goodwood Steps (Spirals) 1994-96
steel, L 32 m
Enabled by the Henry Moore Sculpture Trust and Sculpture at
Goodwood

'*Goodwood Steps* started from a work that I made indoors in Halifax,
Yorkshire, and whilst working on this piece I realised that it would be
quite different from the Halifax work, which was a sculpture inside a
room with a stone floor. Although it was an open form, it was very
enclosed within the room. *Goodwood Steps* is a sculpture against a
landscape. You can get away from it, see it whole, look at it from
above, and you are conscious of the view of the countryside through it
and the big sky. However, the sculpture still relates intimately to the
viewer. Walking along its length and under the steps one gets a kind of
physical experience - something like the way the viewer experienced
The Tower of Discovery which stood at Sculpture at Goodwood for
three years.

'I have been fascinated by the project because it's so architectural.
Because of this the piece seems to bear a different relation to us and
to the environment from what we normally expect of sculpture. The
repetition and mechanical elements are a counterpoint to the grand
view of the downs - not as in the work of Moore, which was often a
reminder of the landscape, but as a contrast to it, much in the way
that the mechanical shape of a windmill brings a human dimension
to the land.'

This statement was made by Anthony Caro at Goodwood whilst he was
working on the sculpture.

Ana Maria Pacheco
Requiem 1986-95
Portland stone, slate, bronze, steel, painted, L 750 cm
Enabled by Sculpture at Goodwood

It is quite natural to surmise what might be contained in a sealed parcel
or a bag. The use of such a device in Ana Maria Pacheco's *Requiem*,
however, serves to make us look elsewhere in the sculpture for clues.
The pile of slates on which the parcel is placed might suggest some,
and the figure, taking a first tentative step away from the ties which
attached him to the earth, his eyes fixed to a far horizon, gives us
more. Here is an enigma. Like much of Ana Maria Pacheco's other
work in sculpture, painting, drawing and printmaking, there is a
narrative involved. Characters which inhabit her carefully woven tales
are frequently depicted making a journey, and the paraphernalia of
travel, a mysterious bag or a box of tricks, is sometimes used in order
to intrigue and tease.

Ana Maria Pacheco began work on the sculpture in 1986, as a tribute
to her father who had recently died. The carving and final form of
assembly were completed at Hat Hill in March 1995 during cold, wet
weather with the artist crouching in considerable discomfort under a
temporary awning in driving rain. The rain persisted and eventually
dissolved the painted stripes on the figure's trunks. Ana Maria Pacheco
came back to Hat Hill to repaint them in the early summer; the sun was
shining and the work was completed. Apparently this was the only time
that she had worked on *Requiem* in good weather.

John Maine
Enclosure 1995
Portland stone, D 244 cm
The Artist

Enclosure is a section of a circular column, three-quarters of the circle being enclosed and one quarter open. Made as part of a series of columns, this was the largest of a group of ten exhibited at Winchester Cathedral in 1992. However, typically of John Maine's working practice, when the sculpture had been standing in his studio for several years after the exhibition, he began to work on it again and developed the piece to its current state - to a point where he considers it to be complete.

During the first half of this decade John Maine was also working on other large sculptures devoted to the column form, most significantly the *Doddington Stacks*, of local sandstone, *Strata*, a 30 metre high granite monument in Japan, and *Chiswell Earthworks*, an enormous landscape sculpture of earth and stone built into the Dorset coast. Some of the qualities in these works are to be found in *Enclosure*, most obviously in the column form, but also in the layers which make the structure, and in the treatment of the outer surface. Here the carved, gently undulating pattern unites the separate elements - not precisely, however, as John Maine likes the viewer's eye to make the final leap and therefore the connection. The point at which *Enclosure* becomes different is in the break of the circular form, the place where the artist reveals the interior space. The inside of the sculpture is rough and weathered, much as the stone would appear when cut from the quarry and left in the open air for a long time. The patina of age, with old quarry marks and cuts made by the artist some time ago, contrasts strongly with the freshly carved and textured exterior, where the diagonal ripples add dynamic movement and take the eye around the form. The outside, it would seem, has become the interior.

Glynn Williams
Gateway of Hands 1992
bronze, H 335 cm
Enabled by Sculpture at Goodwood

This is Glynn Williams's largest sculpture to date, of which there are two casts in bronze. This, the original, welcomes visitors to Sculpture at Goodwood.

The piece is typical of Williams's work, demonstrating his unique blend of figuration and abstraction. He first employed the notion of slicing into naturalistic forms and shifting the pieces into new relationships in *Portrait with Flowers* 1990-91, which was shown at Sculpture at Goodwood during the first season. The dynamism which he found this method of working gave to the forms can be seen in the hands, which from the front look quite realistic, but from behind take on a curious ambiguity. With the hands, the implied movement of opening the palm in a gesture of welcome is underlined by the centre sections of each hand being sliced and swivelled, out in one, slightly inward in the other; pushed forward in one and slightly back in the other. The way in which the hands interact is also curious. Having been parted in the gesture of greeting, they are sited as two separate elements, but the composition remains as one, largely through the continuation of strong diagonals in each which are readily linked by the eye.

Such compositional devices were used by the cubists in their quest for a better understanding of form. In Picasso's *Glass of Absinthe*, he moved portions of the glass and its contents into new relationships to give a whole view: an entire experience of seeing round and within the form. So it is with these hands.

The hands are a self-portrait, undeniably those of their maker.

David Mach
The Wild Bunch! 1996
Fibreglass, tools, Chrysler Jeep, L 390 cm
Enabled by Sculpture at Goodwood

The Wild Bunch! features the model figures of children and animals
which stand in every high street waiting benignly, wistfully, modestly
for alms to be paid through the slot in a proffered box or through a slit
in an ear, head or paw. These meek beings, through Mach's
intervention, have become anarchic, demanding money as they hurtle
along in their Jeep, brandishing weapons in the form of chainsaws,
screwdrivers and hammers - some of the tools which may have been
employed in their construction. Once-simpering dogs now bare their
teeth, a penguin snaps its beak, and a blind child becomes a reckless
joy-rider.

David Mach draws our attention to objects that we may overlook or
take for granted. He turns our perception and assumptions upside-
down to sharpen our response and to get us to look at the world in
another way. Most of Mach's work suggests that there is an alternative
point of view, and sometimes, by the most minimal alteration of the
original materials, meanings can be totally turned about.

The slightly off-balance siting of the Jeep underlines speed, energy and
chaos. It has echoes of a cartoon where velocity is expressed by such
means. This graphic device draws a parallel with the way in which the
figures were originally depicted. They are three-dimensional illustrations
of animal and human kind - generalised rather than specified
representations.

This lively assembly is the antithesis of the original collection of figures,
but there is yet another twist in the tale. It is Mach's intention that *The
Wild Bunch!* should work for a charity, so the sculpture will be sold, and
the proceeds, once fabrication costs have been met, will go to Save the
Children Fund.

Sculpture at Goodwood's Gallery and Reception

The architect of the building, Craig Downie writes, 'When I first visited the copse the sense of timelessness and calm heightened my awareness of the responsibility I had to place a form within a balanced collage of sculpture and landscape. My response, influenced by the rides and undulations of the site, was to create a space that reflected this very directional landscape and that encouraged you to move on to somewhere else, with the impression of the land passing into the space and long views through it.

'The building is set between two avenues with its solid side timber walls forming a continuation of the lines of trees, and is approached from the north by a sloping pathway through large sculptured hands (Glynn Williams *Gateway of Hands* 1992). A green copper wall at the external arrival space is the only vivid colour employed. From here there is a view through the building down a long vista into the copse and a location used for tall kinetic sculptures. The directional effect of the side walls is most apparent, extending with timber broad walks onto the landscape. The east/west axis of the building, an extension of a narrow row of trees, is defined by a large roof light. The north/south axis is a steel goal post, which passes through the side walls.

'Internally, backing onto the green copper wall, a group of three television screens provide the latest digital imaging systems for visitors to access. Apart from the copper, all colours are soft and restrained, which, with the changing light and shade in the surrounding landscape, provides a sensitive backdrop for sculptures to be seen individually.'

Architect: Craig Downie Associates, Main Contractor: D Burgess, QS: Davis Langdon Everest, Engineer: Ove Arup & Partners, Steelwork: Allslade Ltd, Glazing: Parnham Brothers Ltd, Copper Wall: Boss Metals Ltd

Edward Allington

Fallen Pediment (Piano) 1994
copper, L 300 cm
Enabled by Sculpture at Goodwood

This is the only sculpture, so far, that Edward Allington has made to be shown in the open air. He was persuaded to do so by the qualities of light and colour that Hat Hill Copse had to offer, when towards the end of the day on his first visit to the copse the light falling through the trees shed a red glow over the green ground cover and the trees appeared to be as perfect as those in a Japanese garden. His choice of copper for the sculpture is reflected in his first impressions, although it is a metal that he loves and uses frequently.

Elements of architecture and the realm of classicism which are central to Allington's work are here in *Fallen Pediment*, the concept for which at first seemed to be relatively simple. He planned to make a form which appeared to be resting lightly on the ground, with a modest presence that you might miss should you not be looking carefully. When he began to draw the slightly roofed pediment shape, distorted by pulling it round in a horizontal plane, he thought that the resolution would be straightforward. 'I started to try to draw it and although I could make quite reasonable freehand sketches of the way I thought it might be, drawing in a technical manner always failed. I presumed my technical draughtsmanship was not up to it, so I did not worry about it.' However, when he began to work with sheet metalworkers they all began to realise how problematical the construction was going to be. He also made a cardboard structure which failed in the same way as the drawings, but slowly the work was resolved, revealing in the process the tricks that stonemasons employ when carving pediments for buildings.

Trupti Patel
Stay 1995
stone ware, pigment, H 212 cm
The Artist

Stay is a collage of the female body which has been segmented and integrated into an architectural space. The basic structure of the work is an obelisk which is five-sided and is divided into a series of levels and frames from which parts of the body variously protrude, indent or pierce. The polygonal shape allows the viewer to see portions of two further sides whilst studying one. This optical device provides an invitation to look further. Figurative elements may be viewed from the base upwards in a spiralling motion - the foot is shattered, the knee presses out, the stomach is gouged.

In this work Trupti Patel pursues her preoccupation with the human form and its physical and metaphysical context: the woman, the sense of home, feelings of being needed both physically and spiritually. In stark contrast is the implied violence of graffiti and the fissures in the surface. Both are violations, but the word 'Stay' introduces a contradiction which says 'stay within', within the concepts of the home, body, family or self.

Clay is Patel's preferred medium. When working in India she uses terracotta, but in the northern British light she opts for this natural creamy stone ware as it absorbs and reflects light in lively ways. The inherent earthiness of clay is for her entirely appropriate to her subject. The pigment which is rubbed in to the upper sections of the sculpture celebrates the tactile nature of the clay. She has worked this soft porous material with a high degree of sensitivity to the quality of human flesh, making the material at one with her concept. The stabbing, pushing and defacement which is in stark contrast with the gentleness of form and the care in making, serves to underline the drama taking place within the confines of the piece.

Ian Hamilton Finlay
The World Has Been Empty Since the Romans, 1985
Bath stone, steel chain, L 735 cm
Victoria Miro, London

These slabs of stone, resembling fragments from a Roman
archaeological site, with their carefully inscribed words in classical
letter-form, are a very bleak statement. Made in collaboration with
a stone mason, the poem sets up trails of thoughts about European
culture. But is this rhetoric? Is it a metaphor? Finlay proposes the right
sentiment through the most appropriate medium, and we believe that
at Hat Hill, close to evidence of Roman occupation, the sculpture has
found its most fitting place.

The possibility that such fragments may have fallen from the inscribed
architrave of a Roman temple is suggested by the way in which Finlay
has displayed them. Reassembled, like portions of a jigsaw, the stones
are hung in line, not only for the message to be read, but to give
museological overtones which may also underline the philosophical
content of the work.

Lynn Chadwick

Stranger III 1959 (cast 1996)

bronze, L 264 cm

Enabled by Sculpture at Goodwood

One of only a handful of public commissions undertaken by Chadwick, *Stranger III*, originally commissioned by the Air League of the British Empire, gave him an opportunity to work on a monumental scale. This sculpture was to commemorate the double crossing of the Atlantic by the Airship R 34 in July 1919, and was to be placed outside the Long Haul Terminal at Heathrow Airport.

The architect of the terminal, Frederick Gibberd, the Royal Fine Art Commission, the Minister of Transport, Harold Watkinson, and the Committee of the Air League were all enthusiastic about the sculpture. However, in 1958 an opposing committee led by Lord Brabazon of Tara, who called the sculpture a 'diseased Haddock', with the Guild of Air Pilots and Aviators behind him, forced the Air League to withdraw the commission. Lynn Chadwick made one cast in 1959 which has since been destroyed. Of the declared edition of four, one is sited publicly in Spoleto, Italy, another is at Colby College, Bixler Art and Music Center in Maine and a third in Belgium. Sculpture at Goodwood has completed the edition with this cast made at Chadwick's own foundry, Pangolin Editions in Gloucestershire, from a moulding taken from the piece in Belgium.

The winged figure is a development from the maquette, *Stranger II* 1958. The maquette shows two figures merging with the heads looking both to the left and right, symbolising the double transatlantic journey, with spread symmetrical wings. In the final figure Chadwick has foreshortened one wing and tapered the other, whilst maintaining a compositional balance.

Dhruva Mistry
The Object 1995-97
stainless steel, H 400 cm
Enabled by Sculpture at Goodwood

In 1987 Dhruva Mistry made a number of medallions within which he used images of objects such as a chair which he then developed in two different ways, the object as a representation of human presence and as a more organic thing evolving towards human form. This sculpture is a further development, woven with other ideas explored as early as 1976 in works combining the human figure with cubes, which evolved towards the physical content becoming entirely geometrical. Here, the subject is the object, and Mistry plays with that area between the onlooker and the object with the intention of making the onlooker's perception become the content. *The Object* is perceived by looking at it, looking into it, looking round it and looking through it.

The overall quality of the piece is well defined in terms of planes, forms and cut-outs. The planes are meant to work architecturally, and are here combined with an interest in crystalline forms which may be seen through - the roof being a crystal shape which might be read either as a crystal or a roof. The entrance is an invitation into the object/palace/castle/dream-castle where there are signs of welcome, but physical entry is impossible. Any idea of reality is constantly confounded. As the viewer looks at one side of the sculpture expectations are set up, only to be dashed as he/she moves around it.

Dhruva Mistry is very clear about his play on perception. In this sculpture the play on meaning and on language, almost a tease, is taken full distance, with the material quality of *The Object* having equal physical and intellectual weight. Stainless steel, sanded to a mellow silvery surface is, for Mistry, the perfect medium through which to deliver this piece. Treated in this way, steel has an ambiguity that distances itself from the physicality of stone.

34

David Nash
Mosaic Eggs 1995
oak, H 225
The Artist

Only slightly more complex in form than the pyramid, globe and cube which recur time and again in Nash's sculpture and drawings, in a wide range of scale, colour, wood and treatment, the oval or egg has taken its place in his repertoire and has been explored by him in many different ways. Often as sculptures the ovals exist in pairs.

Egg shapes may differ greatly one from another, some longer, some more pointed or blunt, rounder or flatter, stretched, linear or solid. A symbol of fertility with the potential for increase, a form containing inner (possibly unknown) life and energy, the egg as starting point for sculpture offers many possibilities. David Nash has cut eggs vertically with the grain of the wood to form delicate fissures and horizontally against the grain, has cut them regularly and randomly, has carved patterns, reliefs and repeated shapes of mosaic, as in these two oak pieces.

Mosaic Eggs recall Easter eggs from Imperial Russia, decorated with fine jewels; but these are hewn large from massive oaks, with the tessellations represented by deep carving. Robust in form and texture, these eggs sit within the woodland, as much at one with the landscape as fallen fir cones. Their relationship is carefully considered: one on its side, the other vertical, with space to walk between them so that a slightly discordant note enters. The comfortable notion of nestling eggs is excluded, yet the eye draws them together to read the sculpture as a whole. Nash's first piece in a series of egg forms was *Mosaic Egg* 1988.

Keir Smith
Stefano 1997
bronze, H 518 cm
Enabled by Sculpture at Goodwood

St Sigismondo, a Renaissance church in Cremona, provided Keir Smith with the point of departure in developing his ideas for this sculpture. Since he has had a long and academic interest in the art of the Renaissance throughout his career, it may seem surprising that this passion has not surfaced before in Smith's work. This dormant force was unleashed when he made his first visit to Italy in 1989, and on a typically hot and dusty August afternoon came across the church. The cool, dark interior, with light from the high rose window in the west wall pouring into the chapel of Saints Caterina and Cecilia on the northern side of the church, had a significant impact on Smith, and has directly informed the palpable nature of the sculpture. This experience coincided with a period of continual drawing, which from time to time Smith has pursued to the exclusion of working in three dimensions. Drawing in such a concentrated manner, searching for form and content which he could bring together in his sculpture, resulted in *The Cremona Wilderness*, a series of works in watercolour and pencil on paper depicting objects and buildings in barren rocky landscapes.

Stefano emerged from the series, together with another sculpture, *The Tomb of Francesco*, on which Keir Smith has worked concurrently. St Stephen was stoned to death for blasphemy, and the pile of stones viewed beyond the portion of the church, together with the single rock on the altar piece of the sculpture, have become icons for the martyr. The sculpture represents a section through the church of St Sigismondo with its walls dissolved to reveal the cairn of golden stones and the distant landscape. Absorbing the landscape into the sculpture in this way was a theme of Smith's earlier work, which was made almost entirely to commission and in response to particular sites. Here the landscape is incidental, but acknowledged.

John Davies
Head 1997
bronze, H 210 cm
Enabled by Sculpture at Goodwood

In his early sculpture John Davies used a room or exhibition gallery as
a theatre, devising spaces to see how individually made figures worked
together, moving them around as an abstract sculptor might move
stones or wood to form different relationships. Gesture was important
and remains so today, particularly in his drawings, as does the element
of story telling. Davies makes small models or maquettes and life-sized
human figures which relate in tension and narrative, and has now
added exceptionally large heads to his repertoire. For him these new
extremes of scale provide opportunities to explore how the human
figure may be perceived and how we can relate to it differently. The
minute figures with their intense detail endow the viewer with authority.
The large heads, with no less detail in their surface, reduce the viewer
to the stature of a child, where a hand in relation to a face is tiny and
the surface appears to be awesome.

John Davies has spent the last four years working on a group of large
heads in an attempt to get as near as possible to his subject. Two or
three of these massive heads, placed so close together that you have to
squeeze between them would give the sensation of being in a crowd or
they might be like ancient standing stones or massive rocks which were
also faces. These heads pose questions for the viewer about the
relevance of making figures in the late twentieth century, about the role
of figurative sculpture at this time, and about the possibility of knowing
ourselves. Sculpture, in John Davies's opinion, may become a talisman
for the age in which it was made. Looking back at Giotto, for example,
the humanity in his groups of figures, their gesture, iconography and
sculptural form are as relevant now as they were five hundred years
ago. They became a talisman of the early Renaissance, and possibly
these heads may become ours for the end of the twentieth century.

Thomas Heatherwick
Pavilion, 1993
perspex, wood, aluminium, H 400 cm
Sculpture at Goodwood

A twentieth century folly, *Pavilion* shares many qualities of its eighteenth and nineteenth century predecessors. It is a beautiful and curious structure of dubious function. The line and form are sculptural, the materials modern and tested in innovative ways. Like Caro's *The Tower of Discovery,* it is sculpture that can be experienced both from outside and within.

Transparent materials have been used by artists in their sculpture in order that the volume of a form may be experienced without appearing to have massive weight. The work of Naum Gabo and Antoine Pevsner in transparent plastic and wires, and Henry Moore and Barbara Hepworth's stringed figures of the 1930's are early examples. *Pavilion* has most affinity with the stringed sculptures which is evident in Heatherwick's use of line and twist, where he sets up rythmic curves with lines that are in themselves entirely straight.

Pavilion was made whilst Thomas Heatherwick was a student at Manchester. Without sponsorship, in this case from British Alcan and G.E. Plastics, a work of this scale would have been difficult to achieve. However, when the pavilion was on display outside the Business Design Centre in Islington, Wilfred Cass saw it and was attracted by the line and expansive confidence of the piece. He bought it for Hat Hill.

Steven Gregory
Paparazzi 1996
bronze, H 152 cm
Enabled by Sculpture at Goodwood

Groups are seldom benign, whether massed people, flocks of birds
or herds of animals - there is always an element of unease and
unpredictability about them. As with his very successful series, *Bag Men*
1993, which were featured in Sculpture at Goodwood 95/96, this
parade of anthropomorphic cameras gives rise to feelings of revulsion,
horror and humour. The cameras on vultures' legs tell us that they prey
on their victims - such images surely inhabit the nightmares of most
members of the glitterati. The menacing stance of these creatures, their
undeniably black patina giving character to their black souls, is
intensified by their group presence. Hunting in a pack, they survive, but
ultimately this is the survival of the fittest as they seemingly jostle for
position to get the best shot.

Gregory collected ancient stills cameras and a movie camera, finding
them in antique markets and second-hand shops, and used them to
create different characters within this group. Their individuality is
emphasised in different ways: the bellows in one, the placing of the
camera vertically or horizontally in others. After all, we are all unique.
The smallest of these dark beings sneaks to the fore to gain a better
view, the extended claw of one towards the rear menaces both his
colleagues and their prey. The glistening eyes of the lenses, their
penetrating collective eye, serve to emphasise their intent, and are
a subtle but essential touch in this assembly.

Is this a severe case of media bashing? Possibly. More likely a wry
look at a phenomenon of the late twentieth century, a marked sign of
our times.

Bernard Meadows

Large Seated Armed Figure 1963
bronze, H 75 cm
Private Collection

Large Seated Armed Figure is a classic example of Bernard Meadows's work, in subject matter, in the tensions exhibited within the forms and the contrasts between them. It is a confrontational piece, at once aggressive and vulnerable. The blades of knives and spears jut from the sides of the figure which appears to be clothed in a flack jacket. However, the figure is naked but for this slight cover, and his unprotected human attributes leave him as vulnerable as the rest of us. Meadows made other sculptures close in form to this, standing, sitting and armed, first in plaster then cast in bronze.

Another cast of this sculpture belongs to the Keatley Trust and is on loan to the Fitzwilliam Museum, Cambridge.

Other preoccupations throughout Meadows's career have been crab and bird forms, and he has kept largely to these references, and to the human figure, in his sculpture, drawing and collage, however abstract the work might be. These armed figures came a few years before Meadows began working with softer rounded forms, erotic imagery in highly polished bronze, in stark contrast to the awkwardly composed crabs and cockerels, jabbing and squawking.

Andy Goldsworthy

Herd of Arches 1994
sandstone and slate, L 1500 cm (approx)
Michael Hue-Williams, London

The quarry at Gatelawbridge in Dumfriesshire was the site of a work
which is illustrated in *Stone* by Andy Goldsworthy (Viking/Penguin
Books, 1994) under the inscription:

> Out of the quarry
> seven arches
> made over two days
> no failures
> one almost fell -
> slipped down the face of a rock
> as I removed supporting stones

This was the first manifestation of the sandstone arches, made entirely
in the spirit of Goldsworthy's practice of using materials in their place of
origin. The stone from this quarry was used in the construction of major
eighteenth- and nineteenth-century buildings which make up much of
Glasgow, the distinct pink colour lending warmth to the northern
townscape.

This notion of movement found its way into *Herd of Arches*, a group
which seems to have wandered in search of a new location. Sited by
Andy Goldsworthy and Joe Smith at Hat Hill Copse, the *Arches* are
placed along a pathway winding between fairly dense trees, against a
dark green ground-cover of ivy. Here the colour contrast between the
red stone and the green ground lends a strong dynamic to the piece,
which first emerged against its own colour in the rough waste ground of
the quarry.

Paul Neagu
Triple Starhead 1987-93
stainless steel, H 500 cm
Enabled by Sculpture at Goodwood

For Paul Neagu sculpture is a catalyst for ideas and their social role. His works are archetypes for notions that are not normally seen in concrete form. In *Triple Starhead* he has taken the opened up shape of a shooting star and constructed it in three repeated forms firmly bolted together and rooted in the ground. However, the soaring head with its 'comet's tail' (seen clearly during April 1997 with Hale-Bopp in the north-western sky over Britain) conveys meanings quite contrary to those of a heavy earthbound object. The convention of a blurred photographic image capturing a moving body is relevant here, and the 'tail', a graphic device used by cartoonists, acts as a visual thrust whilst in fact being an anchor. The shimmering surface of stainless steel worked to swirling textures endows the material with additional resonance in both sunlight and moonlight, heightening the concepts behind *Triple Starhead*.

In the catalogue for his exhibition *Nine Catalytic Stations*, Serpentine Gallery, London 1988, Paul Neagu is quoted '...Starhead figures release radiance, spiritual and intelllectual energy; sunlight; clarity; Apollonian lucidity. It's turning and upward motion the balletic expression of delight.'

David Mach
The Garden Urn 1996
galvanised wire coat hangers, H 250 cm
Enabled by Sculpture at Goodwood

David Mach employs no end of curious and unrelated materials and
man-made objects in his sculpture. From piles of unused newspapers
and magazines he has fashioned full-scale classical columns; from
rubber tyres, submarines and Greek temples; from match heads, the
most colourful portraits, and from burnt match heads, sombre ones.
It is from the match heads that a series of portraits using wire coat
hangers emerged. The sitter's face was modelled, and the contours
described with closely assembled rows of hangers, the hooks providing
a shimmering aura around the head.

This *Garden Urn* came about because David Mach was interested
in the over-decorated, reproduction garden urns that can be found in
garden centres. Given Mach's long fascination with kitsch items this was
not unusual, but the twist in the tale came when Sculpture at
Goodwood asked him for one of his wire coat hanger garden urns.
He had not made one, but thought this to be a reasonable idea for a
sculpture. We found that the gardens of Biddulph Grange, a National
Trust property in Staffordshire, had the ideal sugar-bowl urn. With the
help of the head gardener, Bill Maleclei, photographs were taken and
the shape and scale approved by Mach. The National Trust's Mercia
Regional Office gave permission for Mach's assistant, Philip Stroud, to
take a copy of the urn, which he made in fibreglass. The fibreglass
version is displayed tipped over, spilling fruits onto the ground, opulent
and extravagant. The coat hangers were laboriously assembled by
Adrian Moakes at his workshops in Manchester. The result is a sculpture
of enormous humour and curious beauty, resplendent in a sylvan
setting, which cocks a snook at our preconceptions and desires for the
status that such objects are supposed to imply.

Bryan Kneale

Deemster Fish 1996
corten steel, L 366 cm
Enabled by Sculpture at Goodwood

Deemsters are the judges of the Isle of Man, who, when reciting how they will carry out the laws of the island, promise to do so 'as evenly as the spine of the herring lies between its flesh'. The herring, historically the staple food of the island's people, has become a symbol of good, and Bryan Kneale, himself a Manx man, has used the form of the herring in this sculpture. He was commissioned by the Deemsters to make a sculpture for their court building in Douglas, and he spent the last eighteen months or so investigating the nature of the fish, and relating it to one of three possible sites in and around the building - a wall, a ceiling and an open outdoor area. He found over fifty possibilities in drawings and in metal models, and decided that a structure to hang on a particular wall in the courthouse was the best solution. The wealth of ideas related to the subject meant that Sculpture at Goodwood was able to help him realise a free-standing version.

Kneale developed the form as an 'inside/outside' structure in which both the exterior and inner workings of the fish were conveyed without being too literal. The many models and drawings he made varied in emphasis from mechanistic, possibly very abstract solutions to others which conveyed more movement. The Goodwood piece is the most abstract. An inclination towards investigating skeleton forms in animals, birds and reptiles is well established in Kneale's vocabulary, and these pieces are both complex and mature.

The model for *Deemster Fish* is exactly like the finished sculpture. Bryan Kneale has a strong sense of scale in his work, which allows his models to be enlarged precisely. The flexibility and resilience found in corten steel allows the form in this sculpture to remain precise - a softer, polished metal would not hold the shapes so exactly.

Charles Hadcock
Caesura IV 1995
cast iron, H 500 cm
Enabled by Sculpture at Goodwood

Caesura: a pause near the middle of a line, or a break between words within a metrical foot, specifically in Greek and Latin poetry. *Caesura* for Charles Hadcock is a series of sculptures in which he explores and celebrates fragmentation, mathematics, multiplicity and the impossible. In *Caesura IV* the two fragments of a single sphere are turned against each other, making it impossible for the globe to be completed. It seems that if the eye were to carry the ascending curves to their conclusion, they would first form an arch, and then complete their circle under the earth. Furthermore, the blocks which form *Caesura IV* are all identical, apart from those at the edges where there are no bolt holes. Their placement suggests that they would complete a globe, but the fact that they do not diminish in size towards the poles makes this impossible. These twists in function are enjoyed by the artist as he alters the mathematics of the form, releases the geometry and then destroys the apparent function.

The plates of cast iron, bolted together with industrial precision, are made to the rules of the Golden Section (the division of a line so that the whole is to the greater as that part is to the smaller part), and in this case are based on the proportions of the artist's body. The outer skin is turned inwards showing the 'industrial' construction of multiple parts, thus turning on its head the logic with which the composition was formed. The textured surface is a celebration of man-made replicas of natural forms, as Charles Hadcock prefers to delve into areas first explored by others, the challenge posed by nature seeming too great. His abiding interest in mathematics, architecture, archaeology, the recent industrial past and manufacturing processes testifies to this.

Log Cabin 1992
Sculpture at Goodwood

Before they cleared the grounds at Sculpture at Goodwood to make spaces for sculptures, Wilfred and Jeannette Cass, knowing that there would be plenty of wood as a result, began to research ways of using it. They also thought that it would be both useful and interesting to have shelters placed in the copse where visitors might rest as they walked round. They knew of the pioneering work carried out by the Parnham Trust at Hooke Park in Dorset, and sought their assistance in realising the first building to be sited in the copse. The log cabin at Sculpture at Goodwood was designed and built by David Hartfield-Dillon in collaboration with Wilfred and Jeannette Cass, as a prototype for relatively low cost, high-tech third world housing. The wood for the outer walls came from the copse, and other materials, excluding the umbrella roof, made by Architen, totalled £800.

Hooke Park College was purchased by Parnham Trust, the charitable educational trust directed by John Makepeace for the scientific use of round wood thinnings which are regularly produced, but rarely used efficiently. Through multidisciplinary two-year courses, the Trust researches, demonstrates and teaches designer-entrepeneurs to design and make quality products from timber. The master plan for Hooke Park includes housing for residential courses, industrial workshops and visitor/information facilities. The Parnham Trust's next phase will focus on ways of applying the innovative technologies, to the development of subsequent buildings aimed at a wider market. These will form a living, working, learning village, based on the sustainable use of indigenous forest resources. Sculpture at Goodwood is keen to pursue the commercial possibilities of this building, and would like to hear from anyone with a serious interest in such a venture.

In the foreground of the photograph opposite is *Tripod Picnic Perch* 1994 by Jim Partridge, on loan from the Contemporary Art Society.

Shirazeh Houshiary

The Extended Shadow 1994
lead, gold leaf, H 400 cm
Enabled by Sculpture at Goodwood

Shirazeh Houshiary's early ambition was to be a writer, and of *The Extended Shadow* she has written: 'The "Heptad" or group of seven was called by Greek philosophers "Minerva" because of its similarity to the goddess in fables, ie it is virgin and unmarried, neither is born from mother (even number) or father (odd number). One could say that heptad proceeds from the "monad" (number one) which is the summit of numbers because it is indivisible by both odd and even numbers. The monad symbolised intellect, male/female and God for the Pythagoreans. Heptad alliance to the monad has made it sacred in many traditions.

'*The Extended Shadow* is a column of four metres in height and constructed of a series of seven sided polygons, ie heptagons, stacked upon each other. These are made of cast lead with the top and underside finished in gold.

'The squaring of the number seven (symbolised by the heptagon) is realised by repeating heptagon forty-nine times in its vertical dimension. Each turns around its centre as they ascend, until a full circle is completed. This act of rotation reveals the inner core of gold and the movement of seven gold lines spiralling upwards around the column. Now one sees the column of density and weight slowly turning to subtleness and light. This process of change is the true meaning of *The Extended Shadow*.'

Bill Woodrow

Endeavour: Cannon Dredged from the
First Wreck of the Ship of Fools 1994
bronze, L 440 cm
Enabled by Sculpture at Goodwood

> The world of fools has such a store,
> That he who would not see an ass
> Must bide at home and bolt his door,
> And break his looking glass. Anon

This is the tenth sculpture in a series devoted to the theme of the 'Ship of Fools', a commentary on the foolishness of mankind wrapped in wry humour. Uncomfortably penetrating insights into human frailty and our seeming inability to learn from experience are all present in *Endeavour*. At first sight the bronze cannon looks real and convincing, a traditional weapon of war with its terrible ammunition placed in a pile close by and ready for use. On closer inspection, however, the image falls apart. The cannon balls are representations of our world. The gun-barrel is the trunk of a tree, sprouting a leafy growth; it is supported by a crouching 'stick' man, sexually well endowed. Potential movement is found to be impossible as the wheels could not possibly work. They are metaphors for aspects of human life. Books represent an accumulation of knowledge from which we seem not to learn and here become dubious supports. A reel of cord, staked to the ground so that forward motion would cause it to unwind, hints at futility. A drum, the skin of which is pierced so that it could not possibly be played, is supported by a spindle which is a burning candle and would soon cease to exist. The last, a tray of food to keep the prisoner alive, has a spindle which is a flute for music to feed the mind. A prisoner? Well, yes, the undercarriage appears to be a prison door. Music sustains us, the prisoner plays a rousing tune on his accordion, the wolf/dog (the head of the man/man's friend?) bites its own leg.

William Pye

Vessel III 1995
bronze, steel, water, H 100 cm
The Artist

William Pye has always been intrigued by getting into his work the most simple effects generated by water. The most basic of all is the meniscus, or 'skin', which forms a kind of 'plateau' in which the water appears to rise above the rim of its container. It is this occurrence that Pye has used in *Vessel III*. Having observed a meniscus, as most of us have done in school science lessons, by filling a glass with water until it almost overflows, Pye wondered why this should not be done on a larger scale. His next consideration was to think how a meniscus, which is essentially a still phenomenon, could be combined with movement but with the slowest possible movement of water. He had seen, at a hydro electric scheme in the Pyrenees, a 'bell mouth weir' which drew water from the centre of the dam in a controlled measure. He was very excited by the shape of the concrete horn through which the water passed, and has employed both the shape and the movement in this sculpture. The difference in level between the central horn and the rim of the bronze vessel is about 7 mm, which allows the water to flow evenly as it is being pumped back to the surface, and this keeps the water level with the rim and maintains the meniscus. Another characteristic of water movement which Pye has employed is that of 'laminar flow': an uninterrupted stream of water flowing along constant streamlines, a phenomenon he had observed in nature. Here a thin film of water glides over the bronze horn.

Bronze was chosen by Pye for *Vessel III* because of its permanence. His preference for a green patina is to do with history and tradition and the fact that he has always enjoyed these connections with the past in his work. The bronze was cast from a plaster form and honed to a fine degree.

Tony Cragg
Trilobites 1989
bronze, H 200 cm
Private Loan

'Sometimes pictures are puzzled together. For example, Darwin's theories and a mass of geological studies have together led to visualisations of trilobite-infested primeval seas and vast tropical forests, dinosaurs, mammoths, and last but not least, man.' Tony Cragg
Artforum March 1988

In *Trilobites* Tony Cragg has taken two motifs, that of the three-lobed body of a marine fossil of Palaeozoic times and a vessel from the laboratory. Neither reference is strange in his work, but the unseen notions that pull this piece together and make it appear as it does are many and varied. Cragg uses a plethora of materials and references for his sculpture, reduced here to a pair of simple primordial forms, but with a wider message. In their original state, trilobites may be around 4 cm in length; here we see them as if under the microscope. They have been enlarged, all the better for (us) to see the form and understand it. But Cragg's sculpture is not straightforward; there is also an underlying threat of unease. The laboratory vessels, set into the surfaces, spoil the simple enlargement, as if a horrible disease has infested the simple creatures. Might it therefore be possible to find here a metaphor for evolution in several ways? The natural, the engineered, or the accidental?

Whichever way we allow our thoughts to wander around the issues addressed in this sculpture, and the possibilities it offers, it is perhaps essential to remember that Cragg is not dogmatic, but is helping us to see more, more clearly.

Kenneth Armitage
Richmond Oak 1985-90
bronze, H 300
The Artist

In the early 1980s Kenneth Armitage took to studying the oak trees in Richmond Park. Fascinated by his subject, he would visit the park weekly, observing the trees through the changes of light, weather and season for a period of ten years. Furthermore, he studied everything he could find in libraries about the English oak and its usage. He made countless drawings, etchings, maquettes and sculptures to his chosen theme, with *Richmond Oak* coming towards the end of this period of intense preoccupation in a culmination of effort, passion and observation. Armitage was obsessed with the subject and gradually realised that he seemed to be unique in his massive response to the oak tree. The forms of oak trees are undeniably sculptural - strong, solid shapes, akin to those he reveals in his work with the human figure. Gesture, an essential component in his studies of the figure, was also to be found in these trees - differently, according to the season: most eloquent in winter, in summer tempered by leaves.

In *Richmond Oak*, what appears to be a park bench encircling the tree trunk began as a circlet of leafy growth and gradually evolved into a seat as Armitage worked the plaster model prior to casting. His rendering of leafy clumps on the top branches is a reflection of the way leaves cluster between the height of summer and the autumn to make masses where light fails to penetrate. In a catalogue for an exhibition in Japan of his oak tree sculptures, drawings and prints, Armitage wrote: 'I like best the late summer when, presumably due to drying and shrinking, the leaves separate into heavy definable clusters; otherwise on certain winter days with a white low mist and each black tree standing free in space isolated and awesome, still, with limbs in frozen gestures.'

68

Richard Long
Six Stone Circles 1981
Delabole slate, D 375 cm
Private Collection

In the 1960s, Richard Long made one of the most significant breakthroughs in the development of British sculpture when he chose to explore the realms of distance and space in a particular way. Not unusual concerns for a sculptor, but the scale of his work, and the way it is recorded, gave new dimensions to sculptural practice. He undertook marathon walks in the most distant and deserted places in the world, and made sculptures relating to those landscapes. A particular part of a terrain would be singled out and a composition involving that view would be made with objects found on the site. Recorded as photographs, maps and short texts, these works have evolved throughout Long's career. He also collects materials which he brings in to the gallery or museum, local materials, possibly, materials that are relevant to the place, and arranges simple circles, rectangles, squares or lines in response to the architecture of the building. His highly developed sense of space ensures a completely satisfying and 'correct' placement and alignment: stones, sticks, lumps of coal, slate, chalk or flint, variously positioned in solid or linear forms.

Six Stone Circles is a slightly different work. Normally Long's outdoor sculpture is ephemeral, useful only until it is recorded, then left for nature to do its worst. Here is a permanent piece sited in an outdoor setting. The Delabole slate from a quarry in Cornwall is arranged in six concentric circles, the larger pieces in the outer circle, the smaller ones at the centre. This sculpture was originally commissioned by Mrs Kieler, on the advice of Dr David Brown when he was a Curator of the Modern Collection at the Tate Gallery. The circles were sited in a wooded part of Mrs Kieler's garden at Kingston-on-Thames. Her collection has since been dispersed, and at Hat Hill we have placed the circles in a clearing in the trees, as instructed by the artist.

William Turnbull

Gate 1972
stainless steel, W 292 cm
Private Collection

The gate form is of great interest to William Turnbull, and he had made two other gates in the early 1960s in stone, bronze and wood. When he made this piece some ten years later, he was thinking about the way that the gate squeezes space. The passage through the gate also held great significance. In Japan and India, for example, you pass through temple gates from the outer bustle of everyday life into another type of space which might be calm, quiet, enclosed or very special. For Turnbull the gate can also be the sculptural equivalent to the window for a painter. 'When you are looking through a window you are seeing a very extensive, infinite space viewed through a very limited compressed space, and it was this particular quality that interested me about doing gates.'

Turnbull chose stainless steel for this particular gate as he was at the time experimenting with the material in other work which was to be shown outside. He enjoyed its reflective qualities, and has emphasised them by his treatment of the surface which he finished with a grinder so that it caught the light in different ways. At this time he was very involved with the effect of light on sculpture and had made a number of works in transparent perspex and some open wood structures which were concerned with how light reflected from or filtered through them. At different times of day or in sunlight or cloud cover, *Gate* can be almost white or uniformly grey.

Gate 1972 forms an entrance to the theatre at Hat Hill Copse, and frames the curving rows of seats and a portion of the stage. It also frames the fields beyond, thus capturing both a specific and an infinite space.

Zadok Ben-David

Conversation Piece 1996
bronze, L 366 cm
Enabled by Sculpture at Goodwood

Zadok Ben-David first made a sculpture on this theme in 1991. This
version is very close to the original, but with subtle alterations. It
is slightly larger, the form is altered to greater dynamism, and the
small figures are in changed relationships. This new version has been
editioned in bronze, whereas the former was made of a metal
armature, aluminium and resin, painted.

In the early 1990s, Zadok Ben-David, who had been making animal
sculptures with human attributes, turned his thoughts towards the
opposite notion: the idea of the beast within man. But there is, in
addition, landscape within the form. The horizontal line drawn along
the back to the head of this crouched figure forms a horizon on which
cavorting figures describe his inner self. Zadok Ben-David has created
something he calls an 'inner-scape'. It is not a self-portrait.

This figure was first made as an outline drawing in metal rods, then
fleshed out with wire mesh and covered with a textured coating of
resin. The inner figures are drawn and cut in aluminium with a jig
saw - 'almost quicker than drawing for me now,' says Ben-David.
In this case, the whole was then cast in bronze.

The silhouette form is typical of Zadok Ben-David's sculpture. It came
from his use of shadows in earlier work, for example, *The Lizard Hunter
Who Has Been Followed by His Own Shadow* and *The Marvellous
Adventure of A Yellow Elephant,* both of 1985. The shadows were just
one element in a work, but have since become the whole sculpture. In
their likeness to shadows, these new sculptures are black and have only
a hint of three-dimensional form.

Langlands and Bell
Fifty Cities 1997
Portland stone, D 600 cm
Enabled by Sculpture at Goodwood

This sculpture, like most works of art, invites us to form ideas about it. Its abstract nature suggests that there is no right or wrong interpretation; but many open-ended possibilities. Here is a seat in a circular plane, made as a boundary or enclosure, and defining a location. Carved into the surface on the horizontal plane are groups of letters forming acronyms for the world's airports. The arrangement is formal although the cities are placed in random order. These fifty places conjure thoughts of travel and all that mass movement of people in the late twentieth century implies: communication, company, isolation, time and change.

When we travel, particularly on long-haul flights, we become out of context and out of 'time'. These landing points, carved in stone, offer definition and context as they become terminals of departure for the imagination. They also suggest routes, although the sculpture is not a compass. The places are terrestrial, the means of moving between them celestial. The more we think into all aspects of this sculpture the more we become aware of its poetry and lyricism and all the elements that pull in the opposite direction. This sculpture explores human activity through the places humans inhabit, their furniture, their buildings and cities, now the globe and next the universe. It is the first work Langlands and Bell have made in stone and the biggest piece so far.

Portland stone, chosen by Langlands and Bell for its hardness and neutral colour, is for them an excellent vehicle for the abstract realisation of their ideas. The precision with which this stone may be cut is also appropriate, as they require formal perfection for organic and disordered subject matter. *Fifty Cities* was carved and installed for Sculpture at Goodwood by Cathedral Works Organisation, Chichester.

Stephen Cox

Granite Catamarans on a Granite Wave 1994
black and white granite, L 800 cm
Enabled by Sculpture at Goodwood

When Stephen Cox first arrived in India in 1985 and travelled to the
coastal village of Mahabalipuram, which is devoted to the production
of traditional Indian temple carving, he was much taken with the
fishing boats that were drawn up on the beach, and which, daily,
plied a hazardous course in the strong currents of the Indian Ocean.
Cox spent several months working with carvers in Mahabalipuram,
preparing his own sculpture for the Sixth Indian Triennale, an
international exhibition held in New Delhi, at which he won a major
prize.

Cox set up his own studio near the sea on the road between
Mahabalipuram and Madras, and has supported a small team of
assistants there ever since. Continuing to be interested in the forms of
the fishing boats, he bought several of them which he kept at his studio
with the thought that one day he might be able to use them. Ten years
later the image of these vessels has appeared in this sculpture. The
granite catamarans are an exact replica of the wooden craft, carved
planks that are bound together with cord. The solution Cox found to
indicate the wave was achieved through drawing with a computer, and
resulted in a grid of vertical columns made to varying heights. Granite
from the quarries at nearby Kanchipuram was selected in two different
colours, black for the boats and white for the wave.

Placed at the edge of Hat Hill Copse, the sculpture refers not only to the
plantation with its even rows of trees, but also to the distant Channel
coastline, as from some angles the boats appear to sit upon the watery
horizon. The sculpture marks a new phase in Cox's development, in
which he appears to be evolving an interest in sculpture as installation.

William Tucker
Frenhofer 1997
bronze, H 210 cm (photograph shows the maquette)
Enabled by Sculpture at Goodwood

The title is taken from Balzac's 1831 story *The Unknown Masterpiece*, later illustrated by Picasso and celebrated by Dore Ashton in her book *A Fable of Modern Art*. In the novel, the painter Frenhofer has for years been engaged in secret on a work which is eventually revealed to be a confusion of colour and line with the model's foot the only recognisable element. The story is a prophetic description of the risks of public incomprehension and of doubt or self-deception on the part of the modern artist.

Tucker's *Frenhofer* is at first sight a formless lump, suggestive of cloud or rock formations, but which on closer inspection seems to resolve itself into a torso, either that of a pregnant woman or of a paunchy male like Rodin's *Balzac* studies. The possibility of many images, and the risk of none at all - of total chaos - is for Tucker a consequence of the art of modelling, with shape and surface generated by the contact of the hand with the soft material. Over the past fifteen years the process of modelling has become as much the subject of Tucker's sculpture as it is the means. Gradually he has sought a more explicit image of the body which is as much sensed internally as from the outside.

Several years ago Tucker was invited by the Henry Moore Institute to work at the studio in Dean Clough. Models and drawings were sent from Tucker's studio in the United States and a preliminary core was prepared. In the event Tucker modelled the sculpture in a brief but intense period in April 1996 in a studio at West Surrey College of Art and Design in Farnham, and Sculpture at Goodwood underwrote the casting in bronze. The location at Goodwood was chosen by the artist for its combination of an intimate space enclosed by trees and the possibillity of longer views.

Bill Woodrow

Sitting on History I 1990-95
bronze, L 300 cm
Sculpture at Goodwood with a grant from The Henry Moore
Foundation

Sitting on History I was purchased in celebration of Sculpture at
Goodwood winning the National Art Collections Fund Prize 1996. This
work brings together in one piece the strands of our main endeavours,
to provide both major sculpture and excellent seating for the interest
and enjoyment of our visitors.

This sculpture was proposed in response to a commission first mooted in
1990, and Bill Woodrow's Tate Gallery exhibition in 1996 gave him
the opportunity to realise one of three ideas for sculptures which could
function as seats. Woodrow had made three maquettes based on a
book form: this version, one with coins as the seat backs, and another
featuring two crows on the spine of the book fighting over a gold coin.
His idea was to have a sculpture that was only completed conceptually
and formally when a person sat on it. *Sitting on History I*, with its ball
and chain, refers not as one might expect directly to chained libraries,
but to the book as the captor of information from which we cannot
escape. All of history is filtered through millions of pages of writing,
making the book the major vehicle for years of research and study.
Woodrow proposes that although we absorb this knowledge, we
appear to have great difficulty in changing our behaviour as a result.

The real books from which the original maquettes were made came
from a box of books given to Bill Woodrow by a London bookseller,
discarded as no longer saleable. To Woodrow's wry amusement, in this
haul were three volumes on the history of the Labour Party, which he
chose to use for the maquettes. Woodrow finds books one of the most
powerful democratic tools in the world and still possibly the most
advanced form of communication - perversely more so than computers
which seem now to dominate our lives.

Peter Burke

Host 1996
reclaimed copper, corten steel H 190 cm
Enabled by Sculpture at Goodwood

This legion of forty cloned figures, identical within, dissimilar without, stand in a mute encounter with their viewers. Their unseeing eyes, incomplete limbs and torsos are formed much as a chiffon scarf might describe features when blown by the wind across a face, or as leather urged and creased into the profile of a Venetian carnival mask over a wooden last. In many ways the fabrication process used by Peter Burke to make *Host* is similar. Burke collected used copper water tanks, and having removed the lime scale, he selected portions to be pressed against two metal press tools, shaped to form the front and back halves of the male human figure. The resulting shells were riveted together to make the whole. The pressure required to make the form 'read' in the copper was so great that it could only be done with an industrial press, in this case with one used in the production of aircraft parts at Dowty Aerospace in Wolverhampton.

But what is this multitude? Why are they here? What are they doing? Turned together, looking at each other, forming intimate groups, they would be benign and social like people at a cocktail party. Facing towards us, emerging en masse from the trees, they are confrontational, threatening, potentially enveloping, even suffocating. A host of angels might be both fearful to behold yet 'good' in intent - possibly this thought can be applied to these humanoid forms. The scale and distribution of the figures matches that of the trees and they work with the horizontality of the landscape rather than against it. The manner in which the figures emerge from the woodland was also important to Burke, as some are barely visible whilst others stand in full view. The organic and the mechanical merge in *Host* through Peter Burke's introduction of chance into the process of industrial replication, an area which he is continuing to investigate.

David Nash
Two Together 1994
charred oak, H 445 cm
The Artist

In a *Family Tree* drawing of 1995, David Nash shows throughout its
spreading branches the genesis and development of his sculptures. The
first charred column, akin to *Charred Column* 1993 which stood at
Sculpture at Goodwood for three years, lay at the heart of the tree.
Developments from that form, which would include the two 'throne'
pieces which comprise *Two Together*, grow from the centre of the family
tree and appear at the tips of the upper branches.

Charring wood turns its organic surface into mineral with a speed that
makes the conversion from wood into coal the epitome of instant
realisation. The process also serves to preserve the form, which in an
outdoor setting within a growing woodland gives contrast to the living
trees. Vessels, spoons and thrones have their place in Nash's repertoire
have the potential to contain an invisible presence. Columns are a
traditional sculptural device. In primitive cultures totem poles were used
for ritual, and tree trunks hollowed out to contain the ashes of the
departed. Narrow columns support flags in celebration or
commemoration. Most have a dual role - the purpose for which they
were made and that as artifact. David Nash's columns, however, are
made solely as works of art. They may refer to these, but they also hold
clues to the artist's involvement with the material, his way of working
with the wood and against it. As works of art they have no practical
function, but they create an intriguing mood for the beholder.

Two Together brings to mind *King and Queen* 1952-53 by Henry
Moore. Moore's sculpture is centred in humanity and celebrates the
material qualities of bronze. David Nash's sculpture suggests absence,
but no less than Moore, he revels in the substance, the thrust, twist,
growth, arrest and transformation of his chosen material.

Eilís O'Connell
Space Emptied Out 1994
stainless steel, corten steel, bronze, H 600 cm
Enabled by Sculpture at Goodwood

Space Emptied Out is a conundrum, a brain-teaser, a riddle even.
Here are three objects, containers, whose presence suggest that they
could hold things, perhaps liquids, in the bronze and corten steel
structures. The basket weave of the stainless steel cord figure could
contain solid things. The fact is, they contain nothing, not even 'space',
we are told. As we think further, however, the forms themselves displace
space by their mere existence. They occupy a specific area and the
spaces between them are particular and consequently
important to the composition as a whole.

The large and varied grain silos of an agricultural landscape can also
be seen at work in *Space Emptied Out*, found, as here, in intimate
clusters.

Of all the sculpture in the copse this alone defies precise description or
analysis. It is indeed a conundrum.

George Cutts
Sea Change 1996
stainless steel, D 1000 cm
Enabled by Sculpture at Goodwood

Imagine that you are swimming in the sea, with the motion of waves causing kelp to sway to and fro. This vision inspired George Cutts to create a series of moving sculptures which captured this kind of motion. *Sea Change* is one of them.

Driven by an electric motor, the curved poles create an undulating movement, causing a change in the space between them as they revolve. The generous, expansive sway in *Sea Change* reflects its organic origin, interesting to contemplate as it is translated through the inorganic medium of stainless steel. The steel poles catch the light as they revolve, again capturing some of the feeling of an underwater world.

George Cutts is an enthusiastic scuba-diver, and has used his observations of sea weed, currents, wave motion and light in many of his sculptures. *The Kiss* 1991, which was exhibited at Sculpture at Goodwood during the first season, was extremely popular with visitors, and whilst it was powered in the same way as *Sea Change*, the more upright poles gave a very different movement - more curving, less swaying than in this sculpture. The motion in both works has a mesmerising quality, much as the tune of the snake charmer's flute mesmerises the cobra.

Paul Neagu
Unnamed (Eschaton) 1997
stainless steel, bronze D 200 cm
Enabled by Sculpture at Goodwood

This sculpture is linked to a series of works started in 1983 which are illustrated in *Reorganisation of Nothing* published by Generative Art Trust, London, in 1996. Paul Neagu has a long-standing interest in eschatology, the theological doctrine concerned with death and final destiny, which for him generates speculative concepts of a cosmological future. In the material form of sculpture the highly reflective surfaces of stainless steel and polished bronze are appropriate vehicles to realise these concepts. Also the form they take - the circle and globe - at once infinite and finite, encourages the viewer to think beyond the physical reality of the work. Neagu writes that he is seeking, 'a transfigurative brightness, a tangible near-perfect paradise. The spheres are all marked with my name, the artist "me" is atomised, dispensable, potentially unstable as all universes are.'

The spheres are prefabricated boules, produced at a factory in Lyons, 'La Boule Integralé'. In this work they are a metaphor for atomic particles, and the fact that they are not made by the artist's hand is his way of depersonalising the subject. When asked about the colour in this sculpture, the warm bronze against the cooler steel, Neagu said that very rarely does he tamper with the natural colour of the materials he uses because he selects them with their natural qualities in mind.

'*Unnamed (Eschaton)* ... helps me to remember a minute golden bracelet made by an Etruscan craftsman (600 BC). I saw it at Villa Giulia in Rome. It contained a couple of hundred tiny lions, about 4 mm each. It also brings to mind a detail of a relief sculpture by Nicola Pisano (born c.1220) in the Duomo in Sienna which contains a small area of about forty portraits, part of the *Final Judgment*. Artists sometimes feel the need to express a preview of paradise... '

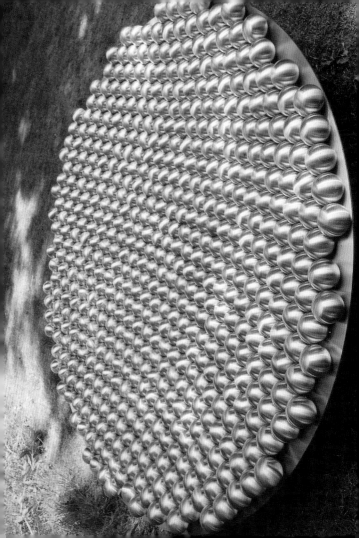

Michael Kenny

In Secrecy and Solitude 1991-92
Portland and Hornton stone (Purbeck stone base), L 200 cm
The Artist

Set with care in a quiet corner of the copse, the circular Purbeck stone base for *In Secrecy and Solitude* takes the place of the gallery floor. Indoors Kenny would have drawn concentric circles on the floor in which to position three geometric forms at random. Here they are placed in considered relationship with the lines incised in the stone base. The sculpture is calm, balanced and harmonious, the physical form giving truth to the spiritual.

Kenny has been working with Portland stone since the early 1980s. He particularly enjoys the contrast between white limestones, and the colourful greens and soft golden browns of Hornton stone which comes from the Midlands, near Banbury, and others which give variety in texture, colour and finish.

Geometry is put to use in many ways in Michael Kenny's sculpture: to define shape in line and volume, to achieve balance and proportion and through this a spirituality, as architects in classical Greece and artists of the Renaissance have done. Line brings together the diverse elements in his sculpture, and the geometry gives tranquillity and calmness.

The notion of movement in such quiet and still work can be found in Kenny's use of the diagonal, a line rising between the horizontal and vertical which might also be the line which holds the composition of the whole in balance.

Nigel Hall
Soglio (Goodwood) 1994
corten steel, L 1100 cm
Enabled by Sculpture at Goodwood

Soglio (Goodwood) 1994 was made some time after Nigel Hall had
visited the Alps, and the site that he has chosen for the sculpture at Hat
Hill reflects similar qualities in that landscape: a gap opening up, a far
view, penetrating and broken forms. The rich patina of oxidised steel
and the geometrically formal shapes contrast dramatically with the
changing landscape. The great subtlety of line and angle to be found
in this piece, Hall's largest sculpture to date, ensures that it rests well
in its space. *Soglio* is the Italian word for throne.

'My work has always been about place, and for Goodwood the
sculpture will echo the fracture in the broken wall,' said Hall, when
planning this work. 'I like the idea of turning back and looking up the
slope of the hill - a sense of engulfing and containment. I am fascinated
by the way geometry can be discerned in landscape, and my preferred
landscapes are mountains or the desert.

'The vertical form is the only vertical in the rolling landscape. It anchors
the sculpture and relates to the viewer's vertical stance. It indicates the
earth's centre. The break in the three wedge forms echoes the angled
break in the long flint wall, while the truncated cone acts both as a lens
and frame to focus and isolate various pockets of landscape.

'It's a meditative space, creating a ground in which the figure of the
vertical can exist in stillness. The sculpture is still when the viewer is still
but active when the viewer moves. For example, when moving across
the face of the sculpture the vertical "knife blade" seems to open and
close suddenly.'

Richard Deacon

When the Landmasses First Appeared 1986
laminated wood and zinc-coated steel, L 750 cm
British Oxygen Corporation

British Oxygen and Sculpture at Goodwood have collaborated in the restoration of this sculpture, and before it is returned to the BOC Headquarters at Windlesham in Surrey, it will be exhibited at Sculpture at Goodwood for two years.

When the Landmasses First Appeared has two distinct elements: the zinc-coated steel frame, and the laminated wooden ribbon which snakes around and through it. The fluid, wandering line of the wood contrasts with the rigid metal enclosure, both in form and in material character. Deacon has made the wood rich in texture, with glue like honey oozing between the laminates, whilst the cool, hard steel is static and remorseless. The freely drawn ribbon is to some extent contained by the metal enclosure, even though the rhythms inherent in the wooden structure suggest a desire to escape.

A sculpture about containment, about movement, this relates in form to other contemporary pieces by Deacon, such as *Blind, Deaf and Dumb* 1985 and *Listening to Reason* 1986. In *When the Landmasses First Appeared*, however, the relationships between the forms, and their relationship to the ground, are much more complex. The lightness and freedom of the wood emerges from and writhes around the mineral element, metal formed originally within the earth's crust. In *Richard Deacon* (Phaidon 1995) the artist is quoted as saying, in conversation with Pier Luigi Tazzi, 'When I began making sculptures the procedures that I used were intended to make the act of work create the form and input structure into the material. Structure and material and form were all equally present on the surface: there was no hierarchy between those elements.' There appears to be no hierarchy within this sculpture.

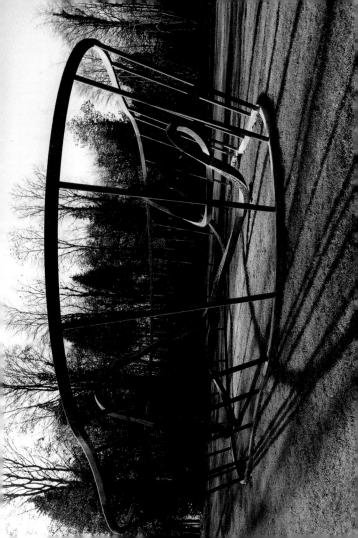

Sculpture at Goodwood Drawings

When Sculpture at Goodwood commissions a sculpture, the artist gives to the foundation a drawing, and possibly a model or maquette related to the work. These not only document the history and development of Sculpture at Goodwood, but also demonstrate aspects of the wide range of contemporary sculptural practice in Britain.

Over the first three years artists have given drawings which range from proposals, technical instructions and interpretations of their sculpture to drawings in which they explore parallel ideas. So far the collection includes works by Edward Allington, Zadok Ben-David, Anthony Caro, Stephen Cox, John Davies, Bruce Gernand, Steven Gregory, Andy Goldsworthy, Charles Hadcock, Nigel Hall,

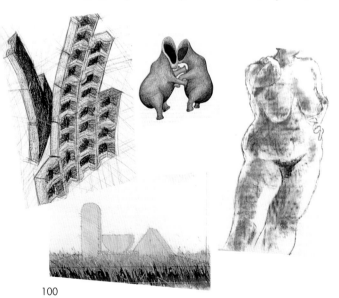

Shirazeh Houshiary, Michael Kenny, Phillip King, Langland Bell,
MIchael Lyons, David Mach, Bernard Meadows, Dhruva Mistry,
David Nash, Eilis O'Connell, Ana Maria Pacheco, Peter Randall-Page,
Keir Smith and Bill Woodrow.

These works form the basis of a growing collection which in time will be
shown for the use of curators and collectors in the Cass's home when that
becomes formally part of Sculpture at Goodwood. In the meantime, they
will form a travelling exhibition which, in addition to the drawings, will
include models, maquettes, photographs of sculptures being fabricated
or cast and a Sculpture at Goodwood Digital Video Disc based on
digital images of sculptors' works.

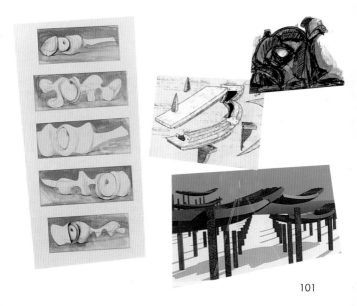

These images have been collected since Sculpture at Goodwood opened in 1994 and help explain the working processes involved. The retrospective sequence of images gives a context, not only to the drawings in the exhibition, but to the sculptures commissioned by Sculpture at Goodwood.

Computer technology is also used in the realisation of ideas for sculpture, and the iris print of Stephen Cox's *Granite Catamarans on a Granite Wave* 1995 is the first in the collection to demonstrate this way of working with the programme form.Z. Grenville Davey is currently exploring with us possibilities for a new sculpture using similar technology.

The travelling exhibition, starting in 1998, will inevitably be open ended, allowing us to add items as more drawings are donated. This collection also forms a basic group of works on which curators of museum and gallery collections may wish to build their own exhibition, an involvement which would be welcomed by Sculpture at Goodwood.

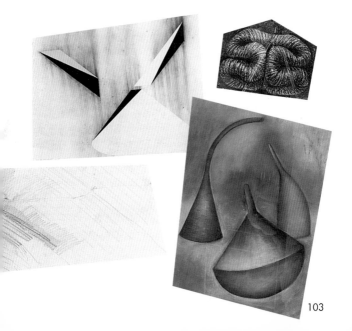

Sculptors' Biographies

Edward Allington

Edward Allington was born in Troutbeck Bridge, Westmorland (now Cumbria) in 1951. He studied at Lancaster College of Art (1968-71), the Central School of Art and Design, London (1971-74) and the Royal College of Art, where he read cultural history (1983-84). He was prizewinner of the John Moore's Liverpool Exhibition (1989) and Gregory Fellow in Sculpture at Leeds University (1989).

Allington's first solo exhibition was at 1b Kensington Church Walk, London, in 1977. Since then his work has been shown frequently in both mixed and one-man exhibitions in many countries, including Japan, America and throughout Europe. He lives and works in London.

A long-standing interest in Greek and Roman cultures is evident in Edward Allington's sculpture and drawing. References to architectural detail, collectors' artifacts, placement and social context also play their part, and the viewer soon realises that there is a sense of deep enquiry as well as a little mischief at play. In his early work Allington explored a wide variety of materials, but recently he has used copper and bronze, sometimes with other elements, such as photographs of the work in a non-museum context.

Kenneth Armitage

Kenneth Armitage was born in Leeds in 1916. He studied at Leeds College of Art (1934-37) and at the Slade School of Fine Art, London (1937-39). During the war years he served in the army and in 1946 became Head of Sculpture at Bath Academy of Art, Corsham, a post which he held for ten years. In 1956 he was awarded the first prize in the International War Memorial Competition in Krefeld, Germany, and in the 1958 Venice Biennale he won the David E. Bright Foundation Award. In 1964, he was Visiting Professor at the University of Caracas, Venezuela, at Boston University, Massachusetts in 1970, and from 1974 to 1979 was visiting tutor at the Royal College of Art. These international aspects of his career reflected Armitage's growing reputation as one of the leading British sculptors of his generation. From the early 1950s exhibitions of his work could be seen in the United States, Europe, Japan and South America, with group exhibitions ranging even wider. Three retrospective exhibitions held at the Whitechapel Art Gallery, London (1959), Artcurial, Paris (1985) and the Yorkshire Sculpture Park (1996-97) have summarised Armitage's achievement and his passions for the human form and human condition, movement and trees. His inclination as an artist has always been towards abstraction and simplification of form, with bronze a preferred medium. His work is represented in public and private collections world-wide. Armitage was awarded the CBE in 1969.

The movement and energy in Kenneth Armitage's sculpture is an abiding presence. Manifest in *People in the Wind* 1950, a sculpture acquired by the Tate Gallery, in which a cluster of four figures strain against the element, this force appears in different form with *Garden Game* 1983 where figures cavort and play against a dividing screen. Armitage writes, 'Naturally my sculpture contains ideas or experiences other than those that derive directly from observation of the human image, nevertheless it is always dressed in some degree in human form.' Parallel themes occur in his drawings and prints.

Zadok Ben-David

Zadok Ben-David was born in Bayhan, Yemen, in 1949, and was brought up in Israel. He studied at Bezalel Academy of Art and Design, Jerusalem (1971-73), Reading University (1975) and St Martin's School of Art, London (1976). When he moved to London to study he not only had to come to terms with a new verbal language, but also a new visual language - British abstraction and conceptual art of the 1970s was very different from that in Jerusalem. At that time, leading British sculptors such as Anthony Caro, Phillip King and Tim Scott were teaching at St Martin's. After two intensive years of study, Ben-David found himself alone in a Greenwich studio and felt the need to come to terms with his own identity through his work - a search for meaning rather than working intuitively. He acknowledged everything that he found in his adopted culture, but selected carefully those aspects that would bring greater meaning to his work as an artist.

Colour and animal forms are characteristic of Zadok Ben-David's early work. The remembered warmth of the Yemeni desert comes through in warm yellows and reds, and the animals, recalled largely through childhood stories, play out their mythical tales. Textured surfaces absorb the light and help the colours to resonate, and the contrast of matt black shadows enable the forms to flatten. In recent work the role of the animal has altered. Instead of examining anthropomorphic animal activity, Ben-David has turned to looking at the animal in man. Man's beastly qualities are indicated by his stance and actions. Metaphysics has drawn Ben-David to an interest in the alchemist and man's scientific discoveries in the eighteenth and nineteenth centuries. Scientific book illustrations from this time also hold a great interest for him, and have found their way into his installation work. All of these focus on an underlying interest in man, his humanity and his progression in the world.

Peter Burke

Peter Burke was born in London in 1944. On leaving school he entered a student apprenticeship with Rolls Royce, Bristol (1960-65), then trained as a teacher at Bristol Polytechnic (1965-68) and studied for one year in the Fine Art Department there (1972-73). Whilst working as a teacher of art and design Burke maintained his practice as an artist, and for the last five years has given his time fully to his work as a sculptor.

The human form has long been a preoccupation in his work, and is expressed in many ways in his sculpture - fragmented, whole, in groups or singly. Burke's engineering background has given him an interest in industrial working methods and structural systems which he incorporates into his work. He enjoys replication and mass production and employs these processes. In his work the random meets the controlled and precision encounters chance.

Drawing is important to Burke as a way of working up ideas for sculpture, envisaging relationships between his figures rather than their full form which takes its chance in the making.

Peter Burke has exhibited his work since 1973 in mixed shows, his first being the Cheltenham Festival's exhibition of sculpture in the open air. His first solo exhibition was at South Hill Park, Bracknell (1978), since when he has shown regularly at international art fairs and in British and overseas galleries. Peter Burke is represented by the New Art Centre Sculpture Garden and Gallery where he has shown his sculptures since the early 1990s.

His work is in private collections in Britain, Europe and the United Sates, and has also been acquired by the Contemporary Art Society, London (Henry Moore Foundation purchase). Peter Burke lives and works in Bradford on Avon, Wiltshire.

Sir Anthony Caro

Sir Anthony Caro was born in New Malden, Surrey, in 1924. He studied engineering at Christ's College, Cambridge (1942-44). After National Service with the Fleet Air Arm of the Royal Navy (1944-46), he attended Regent Street Polytechnic Institute, London (1946) and the Royal Academy Schools, London (1947-52).

Caro worked as a part-time assistant to Henry Moore (1951-53), and taught part-time at St Martin's School of Art, London (1952-1980). There he virtually formed what was to become an influential Department of Sculpture where young artists, following his lead, were working in new materials such as plastic and fibreglass as much as, or more than steel. Caro's early sculpture was figurative and expressionistic, worked in clay and cast metals. In 1959 he broke away from figuration and made works from scrap steel girders and sheet metal, welded and bolted together. Many were coated with industrial and household paints. His first table sculptures were made in 1966. Smaller than previous work, these reclaimed the pedestal in a different form and were made well into the 1980s. Meanwhile he was developing his work in steel on a massive scale, some of which is essentially architectural. In 1993 Caro returned to working with clay in combination with metal and wood (having worked twice before with clay and ceramics) in a series of sculptures describing the Trojan Wars, his first semi-figurative work since the 1950s.

Anthony Caro has had numerous exhibitions throughout the world, from the first *Biennale des Jeunes Artistes* in Paris in 1959 where he won the sculpture prize, to his magnificent retrospective exhibition at the Trajan Markets in Rome in 1993. His work is well known and respected from the United States to Japan, and in 1995 a large retrospective exhibition was shown at the new Metropolitan Museum of Art in Tokyo, the museum's first exhibition offered to a foreign artist. He was awarded a knighthood in the Queen's Birthday Honours 1987.

Lynn Chadwick

Lynn Chadwick was born in London in 1914. He attended the Merchant Taylor's School, and after taking his School Certificate stayed on to study drawing, watercolour and oil painting. He was then sent to Vouvray to study French. From 1933 to 1939 he trained and worked as an architectural draughtsman in London.

In 1940-41 he worked as a farm labourer and then volunteered for the Fleet Air Arm, becoming a pilot and gaining a commission. After the war he returned to his work with the architect Rodney Thomas, specialising in exhibition design. His early sculptural works took the form of mobiles, which he began to make in 1947, having moved from London to Gloucestershire. A mobile constructed from aluminium and balsa wood was shown at the Aluminium Development Stand at the Builders' Trades Exhibition that year. At this time, and until 1954, he produced textile, furniture and architectural designs.

Chadwick's first one-man exhibition was held at the Gimpel Fils Gallery, London, in 1950, the first of many exhibitions world-wide. These have included the XXVIII Venice Biennale of 1956 where he won the International Sculpture Prize, one of many awards and accolades, including the CBE in 1964. Early in his career he worked occasionally to commission, but less as he became established.

His approach to making sculpture is based in construction rather than modelling. Chadwick first makes a linear armature or skeleton before building on a solid skin. The work might be unique or made to a predetermined edition by casting or fabrication. Chadwick has created a permanent exhibition of his work at his Gloucestershire home, Lypiatt Park, and also a foundry, Pangolin, which casts not only his sculpture but also work for many other artists.

Stephen Cox

Stephen Cox was born in Bristol in 1946. He studied at the Central School of Art and Design, London (1966-68).

Cox's work is based in other cultures. Rooted in classicism, his early sculptures related to architecture and archaic fragments, and were realised in stone from Italian quarries. The Mediterranean as the cradle of civilisation of the Western world provided the context and the substance for his work.

In 1986 Cox represented Britain at the Sixth Indian Triennale in New Delhi. He went to Mahabalipuram, a centre for traditional Hindu carving, to make sculpture for the exhibition, and since that time has maintained a studio there. The carvings he made in granite from the ancient quarries of nearby Kanchipuram were to have a great bearing on his work over the next decade. Some were more overtly 'Indian' than others, and might be viewed as being linked to the humanism of both the Eastern and Western worlds.

Another opportunity for Cox to work in a new context, this time in Egypt, presented itself in 1988. He was commissioned to carve sculpture for the new Cairo Opera House, and was allowed to quarry Imperial porphyry at Mons Porphyrytes in the Eastern Desert, which had not been used since the Renaissance. This in turn led to new developments in his imagery, such as references to the human torso. In varying his treatment of the rich red and green stones, Cox developed his sculpture towards a more abstract state. In 1993 he completed a commission for the parish church of St Paul, Harringay, using Italian and Egyptian stones.

Cox continues to work in Egypt and has been given permission to quarry stone from another ancient site, the Kephren Quarries in the Western Desert of southern Egypt.

Tony Cragg

Tony Cragg was born in Liverpool in 1939. He worked as a laboratory technician at the Natural Rubber Producers Research Association (1966-68) before attending Gloucestershire College of Art and Design, Cheltenham, and the Royal College of Art, London (1973-77). Tony Cragg has lived and worked in Wuppertal, Germany, since 1977.

An artist of great international acclaim and immense energy, Cragg has developed more possibilities in the making of sculpture than any other sculptor since Moore discovered the 'hole' as positive space. He has employed more materials than most, and tested them to their limits through a wide variety of means, so that he seems to be one hundred sculptors at any one time. However, the continuum in his work is strong and uncompromising. His concerns are for humanity, its direction, the life of our planet and its projected evolution. Cragg's contribution to the debate on contemporary sculpture practice is considerable, and has yet to be measured.

Early works of the 1970s were mostly made with found objects through which Cragg questioned and tested possibilities. Later pieces, sometimes derived from found materials, demonstrated a shift of interest to surface quality and how that could be manipulated, and a play with unlikely juxtapositions of materials. Results vary from the exquisite to the grotesque, from the refined to the crude, in bronze, steel, plastic, rubber, glass, wood, plaster and more.

George Cutts

George Cutts was born in Rugby in 1938. On leaving school he worked at Goole Shipyard, and whilst there qualified to attend art school. He studied at Doncaster School of Art (1956-58) and at the Royal College of Art, London (1958-60), under John Skeaping.

He has taught at the Royal College of Art, the Royal Academy Schools, Chelsea and Ravensbourne Schools of Art, Trent and Portsmouth Polytechnics, but now devotes all of his time to making sculpture. He has exhibited in Europe and America, and has undertaken many public commissions in Britain and abroad.

Of his work, George Cutts writes: 'I work directly in stone and stainless steel, the opposing materials with such diverse textural qualities interplay, emphasising my ideas. I am mainly influenced by landscape, although many forms subconsciously revert back to the shipyard, for example, large propellers, ribs, curved forms. The mobiles are derived from water movement and are carefully timed to calm and tranquillise the viewer.'

John Davies

John Davies was born in Cheshire in 1946. He studied painting at Hull and Manchester Colleges of Art (1963-67), after which he spent two years at the Slade School of Fine Art, London. He was awarded a sculpture fellowship at Gloucester College of Art in 1989 and in the following year he won the Sainsbury award. The most important solo exhibition for John Davies in his early career was held at the Whitechapel Art Gallery, London in 1972, followed by another at the same venue three years later. His most recent exhibition was at the Whitworth Art Gallery, University of Manchester, in 1995-96. His sculpture and drawings have been included in many group exhibitions in Britain, Europe, America, India, Australia and Japan with pieces being acquired in most of those countries for both public and private collections.

John Davies' sculpture and drawings are centred on the human figure. He has written, 'People are our whole world, sun, moon and stars.' Early figures were often arranged in carefully positioned relationships, playing out a silent drama through look and gesture. Gesture remains important in his single figures, where an extended hand or slight inclination of a head might indicate another presence. The presence of others may also be suggested by a small hand against a large face or several hands joined together. Heads, from small pieces that can be held between two fingers to giant heads like huge rocks, eroded by the wind and sea, demonstrate his skill with scale and drawing. Finely delineated features and well-worked textures indicate character and feeling(s) and many other aspects of the human condition.

The artist's own words best sum up his continued fascination with and explorations of the human form: 'My work has carried me closer to people - in a kind of circle. My sculpture seems to have that function for me. If it does the same for other people that would mean a great deal to me.' John Davies lives and works in Thessaloniki in northern Greece.

Richard Deacon

Richard Deacon was born in Bangor, Wales, in 1949. He studied at Somerset College of Art, Taunton (1968), St Martin's School of Art, London (1970-73) and the Royal College of Art (1974-77) where he gained an MA in Environmental Media.

Working both on a domestic and monumental scale, Richard Deacon combines the essence of human form with elements of engineering in his precisely made structures of wood, metal and occasionally, plastics. Metals are riveted together in sweeping shapes which refer to both inner and outer parts of the anatomy, and wood is laminated, bent and twisted into unlikely ribbons and smoothed to solid perfection in more volumetric states.

Public commissions in many countries have given Richard Deacon opportunities to work on an immense scale. *Moor* 1990 at Victoria Park in Plymouth sits high next to a bridge, and is 247 metres long. He also makes works for a particular occasion, for example objects which are used in contemporary dance performances. In 1993 he collaborated with Hervé Robbe in *Factory*, designing the sets and, with Dominique Fabrègue, the costumes. The dance was performed at La Ferme du Buisson, Paris, before touring France. Deacon's use of performance in his work has undergone change throughout his career. He actively participated in his earlier works but eventually found his physical presence became unnecessary. His work evolves with his thinking, in that he does not establish a set of rules or problems to be solved through a predetermined pattern - the ideas rove with the making process.

Richard Deacon has exhibited widely throughout the world with solo exhibitions, and in significant international surveys such as *Documenta IX* in 1992. He was awarded the Turner Prize in 1987. He lives and works in London.

Ian Hamilton Finlay

Ian Hamilton Finlay was born in Nassau, Bahamas, in 1925. As a child he was brought to Scotland, where he attended boarding school. His education ended at the age of thirteen, when at the outbreak of war he was evacuated to the Orkney Islands.

A short spell at art school in Glasgow was followed by a period in London before Finlay joined the army in 1942. At the end of the war, he worked as a shepherd, studied philosophy, and began to write short stories and plays, some of which were broadcast by the BBC.

Much of Finlay's work has been made in collaboration with other artists and with artisans, and draws on his experience of rural life and the sea. His studies of classicism and ancient philosophers have enriched his work immeasurably.

At Stonypath, near Edinburgh, his home since 1966, Finlay has developed the garden to feature his concrete poetry and sculpture. Although he has gained a considerable international reputation through numerous exhibitions abroad, Ian Hamilton Finlay never travels away from his home.

Andy Goldsworthy

Andy Goldsworthy was born in Cheshire in 1956 and was brought up in Yorkshire. He studied at Bradford College of Art (1974-75) and Preston Polytechnic (1975-78).

After leaving college Goldsworthy lived in Yorkshire, Lancashire and Cumbria. He moved over the border to Langholm, Dumfriesshire, in 1985 and to Penpont one year later. This gradual drift northwards was due to a way of life over which he did not have complete control. However, contributing factors were opportunities and desires to work in these areas and reasons of economy.

Throughout his career most of Goldsworthy's work has been made in the open air, in places as diverse as the Yorkshire Dales, the Lake District, Grize Fiord in the Northern Territories of Canada, the North Pole, Japan, the Australian outback, St Louis, Missouri, and Dumfriesshire. The materials he uses are those to hand in the remote locations he visits: twigs, leaves, stones, snow and ice, reeds and thorns. Most works are ephemeral but demonstrate, in their short life, Goldsworthy's extraordinary sense of play and of place. The works are recorded as photographs. Book publication is an important aspect of Andy Goldsworthy's work: showing all aspects of the production of a given work, each publication is a work of art in its own right.

Some recent sculpture has a more permanent nature, being made in stone and placed in locations far from its point of origin, as for example *Herd of Arches* 1994. The series of chalk *Arches* made at Sculpture at Goodwood in 1995 are semi-permanent, given the fragility of the material, and are now sited indoors at Goldsworthy's studio in Dumfriesshire, to extend their life.

Steven Gregory

Steven Gregory was born in Johannesburg, South Africa, in 1952. He studied at St Martin's College of Art, London (1970-72), returning there to complete his BA (Hons) (1977-79). During the intervening years he was an apprentice stonemason to the company Ratty and Kett, working at Westminster Abbey and Hampton Court. He obtained City and Guilds Craft and Advanced Craft Certificates in stone masonry (1975 and 1976). In 1977 he won the Worshipful Company of Masons Prize.

Gregory chose this course of action because of his desire to learn how to use tools. In the early 1970s art schools in Britain devoted much time to the exploration of concepts in preference to developing craftsmanship, which Gregory found frustrating. Leicester Museum and Art Gallery purchased a sculpture from his BA exhibition at St Martin's, and at that time he was commissioned to make a work for Rio Tinto Zinc using machine tools produced by the company.

Stone carving features largely in Steven Gregory's sculpture, although he has also developed ideas in bronze and other media. His intention is to make work that cannot be disregarded, which sometimes results in harrowing images of the human condition. There is also a lighter side to his work where his humour emerges, although the viewer should still search in the shadows for there might still lurk the black dimension.

Charles Hadcock

Charles Hadcock was born in Derby in 1965. He studied at Gloucestershire College of Arts and Technology (1984-87) and at the Royal College of Art, London (1987-89). His degree show at the Royal College generated a good deal of interest in his work, and many encouraging comments in the press. The ideas he was then trying out in his sculpture - using multiple images and explorations of the ready-made - remain important in his work today. A background in engineering (his father was an engineer), an abiding interest in Victorian engineering and in mathematics have enriched those original preoccupations, and are all present in his current work. His is not entirely a cool and calculated art, but one that also has analogies with poetry and music.

Transformation also plays its part. Polystyrene packaging might be cast in bronze and repeated as a multiple (it is a multiple in the first place), artificial paving stones - mass produced - are found giving texture and repetitive form in some sculptures. The nuts and bolts of nineteenth-century engineered bridges are celebrated in his work, giving the underside of the sculpture equal importance with the rest. Geometry also plays a part, in particular the Golden Section, based on the coordinates of Hadcock's own body, as do the rhythm, pause, crescendos and calm of music. All of this culminates in bronze or cast iron. Hadcock uses factory casting for his sculpture in preference to fine art foundries, as he likes the basic qualities of the factory processes to come through in the sculpture, and in particular revels in the qualities of cast iron.

Charles Hadcock has exhibited regularly in group shows since 1987, and has had one-man exhibitions at 249 Long Lane, London (1991), the Crypt Galley, London (1992) and Reeds Wharf Gallery, London (1996). His work can be seen at BAA Gatwick Stirling Hotel, Melbourne Science Park, Cambridgeshire, ICI, and Allied Domecq.

Nigel Hall

Nigel Hall was born in Bristol in 1943. He studied at the West of England College of Art, Bristol (1960-64) and the Royal College of Art, London (1964-67). On graduating from the Royal College, Hall won a Harkness Fellowship, and until 1969 he lived and worked in Los Angeles, travelling in the USA, Canada and Mexico. His work is represented in numerous public, corporate and private collections in Britain and abroad. Hall's first one-man exhibition was held at the Galerie Givaudan, Paris, in 1967. It is interesting to note that fifty out of his seventy-two solo exhibitions held between 1967 and 1996 have been in galleries abroad in cities spread throughout the globe: New York, Los Angeles, Perth, Melbourne, Sydney, Tokyo, Zurich, Dusseldorf, Cologne and Rome, to mention only a few. This international exposure has led to his work being represented in around 100 public and corporate collections and numerous private collections abroad and in Britain.

In 1970 Nigel Hall produced his first tubular aluminium sculptures in which he explored ways of encapsulating space in a linear manner, thus manipulating our perceptions of it. A sense of place and placement have always been integral to his work, and shadows play a role equal to that of line, mass or void, as do changes of aspect from altered viewpoints. An almost minimal refinement and economy of means in Hall's work has recently given way to robust forms which still remain very carefully considered in their configuration. These refer obliquely to mountain landscape which alters dramatically when the viewer moves within it. Site specific projects have also featured regularly during Nigel Hall's career. These include a wall sculpture for the entrance to the Australian National Gallery, Canberra, 1992; a two-part wall relief in painted and gilded wood for the entrance of Providence Towers, Dallas, 1989; and a free-standing steel sculpture for the entrance to Thameslink Road Tunnel, London Docklands, 1993, his largest structure to date.

Shirazeh Houshiary

Shirazeh Houshiary was born in Shiraz, Iran, in 1955. She studied at Chelsea School of Art, London (1976-79) and then for a year was junior fellow at Cardiff College of Art. Her first solo exhibition was held at the Chapter Arts Centre, Cardiff, in 1980, since when she has exhibited regularly in solo and mixed exhibitions in Britain, Europe and America. Houshiary was nominated for the Turner Prize in 1994.

Her sculpture is rooted in the mysticism of Islamic culture, in particular Sufism, but demonstrates a quest beyond cultural limitations. Treading as she does the path between poetry and the material world, Houshiary achieves an energy in her work which assumes inner light and outer strength.

nb The Sufi movement originated in the 7th century, when Syrian Moslems influenced by Christian mystics, organised monastic houses. Despite vigorous opposition from traditionalists, Sufism introduced into Islam a saintly heirarchy, a strong asceticism and a lush poetry in which philosophical intent was clothed in the language of earthly passion.

Michael Kenny

Michael Kenny was born in Liverpool in 1941. He studied at Liverpool College of Art (1959-61) and the Slade School of Fine Art, London (1961-64). Throughout the 1970s he was a visiting lecturer at the Slade School and from 1983 to 1988 was Head of the Fine Art Department at Goldsmith's College, London. Since he graduated from the Slade, Kenny has had many solo and group exhibitions in Britain and abroad, including Europe, USA, South America, Japan, Hong Kong and Australia. Consequently, many public and corporate collections throughout the world hold examples of his work.

The creative acts of drawing and making sculpture seem, in Michael Kenny's work, to be indivisible. The physical qualities of line are to be celebrated, whether drawn on smooth or textured paper or across a piece of stone, whether made in graphite or coloured pigment. 'Drawing', for Kenny, 'is a means of understanding, of searching for order out of chaos through images.' Geometry, symmetry and asymmetry are concerns, both in drawing and in sculpture. Stones with differing qualities are sometimes brought together in one piece, the grainy dark greens and browns of Hornton stone contrasting with the cool, smooth texture of Portland stone or the warmer hue of Bath limestone. Recently Kenny has introduced blue-grey Killkenny marble and white Carrara marbles into his compositions, adding to the range of colour and surface quality in his sculpture. Strong diagonals and verticals in both solid form and in line, pull our attention towards the notions of gravity which are also vital in his work.

Michael Kenny was elected Associate of the Royal Academy in 1976 and Royal Academician in 1986. He lives and works in London.

Bryan Kneale

Bryan Kneale was born in Douglas on the Isle of Man in 1930. His early ambition was to be a painter, and he studied at Douglas School of Art (1947) and at the Royal Academy Schools (1948-52). In 1948 he won the Rome Prize, and spent most of his time travelling in Italy where he was greatly influenced by the work of the Futurists and metaphysical painters. On his return to London in 1951 he started painting with palette knives with a desire to construct in paint, the foundation of his gradual move towards working entirely in three dimensions. In 1960, having learnt welding techniques, Kneale abandoned painting and had his first exhibition of sculpture later that year.

Bryan Kneale has mostly constructed, forged and cast his sculpture himself. He has taught sculpture at the Royal Academy Schools, Hornsey College of Art and the Royal College of Art, where he was Senior Fellow in 1995, the year of his retirement.

His work is largely centred on organic form. Skeletons and joints of animals are explored through drawing and construction in metal. Kneale prefers to work directly in metal rather than modelling in an intermediary material before casting in bronze.

Exhibitions include regular one-man shows since 1953 and group exhibitions since 1961. Kneale has shown mostly in Britain, with occasional exhibitions abroad, although his work is represented in collections from Australia and New Zealand to Brazil and New York. In Britain his drawings can be found in the Natural History Museum and the British Museum, and his sculpture at the Tate Gallery and in many municipal and private collections.

Bryan Kneale was elected ARA in 1970 and Royal Academician in 1974. He lives and works in London.

Langlands and Bell

Ben Langlands was born in London in 1955 and Nikki Bell, also in London, in 1959. They both studied fine art at Middlesex Polytechnic (1977-80), from which they graduated as Langlands and Bell.

Langlands and Bell sculptures and wall pieces are based in architecture, the history of places and associated human activity. In their work the organic nature of human history and activity is distilled into refined interpretations of architectural ground-plans, made in three dimensions in black, white or monochrome. Some pieces are made in diptych or triptych form and interpret the serial uses of a site, or combine a number of buildings to reflect the differing uses or activities associated with them. Churches, prisons, corporate headquarters, art galleries, museums - everywhere that man inhabits may become a possibility for making sculpture.

They distil and interpret only the essential components of their anthropological source material. In their second solo exhibition, *Traces of Living* at Interim Art, London, in 1986, tables and chairs made in the form of vitrines, topped with glass and contain a dead rat petrified to the point of being leather, old books and broken crockery approximated to a portrait of Whitechapel in the East End of London, where they live and work. These collections provide the point where imagination and speculation take over.

Langlands and Bell have had regular solo exhibitions in Britain and abroad throughout their career, and their work has been included in numerous mixed exhibitions. Their touring exhibition *Langlands and Bell Works 1986-1996*, first shown at the Serpentine Gallery, London, has travelled to Bielefield, Germany and Palermo, Sicily. In 1997, their work is included in *Architecture as Metaphor* at the Museum of Modern Art, New York, and in the central exhibition *Future, Present, Past 1967-1997* at the 1997 Venice Biennale.

Richard Long

Richard Long was born in Bristol in 1945. He studied at the West of England College of Art, Bristol (1962-66) and at St Martin's School of Art, London (1966-68).

As early as 1964 Long made his first work involving landscape. By 1967 he was using the concept of distance, in the form of long walks, and space which he modified in subtle ways. The element of time became important as he made sculptures by walking, hitch-hiking or bicycling on a predetermined route which might be described as a line or circle on a map. The records of these walks exist as maps, photographs and short, descriptive texts. He has travelled the world making his work, in the Americas, Europe, Africa, Nepal, Australia and Japan - a solitary occupation, on occasions involving great hardship and discomfort.

Long's work is highly regarded and he has held many significant one-man exhibitions throughout the world. In 1976 he represented Britain at the Venice Biennale with an installation in the British Pavilion made of marble selected from an Italian quarry.

His practice of making installations in poetic harmony with the buildings in which they are placed has led Long to work in such diverse venues as the Henry Moore Studios at Dean Clough, Halifax, with pieces of coal arranged in a dense black circle, and in 1994, the São Paulo Bienal, Brazil, where he used mud from the Amazon splashed in controlled sweeps on the gallery surfaces. In 1989 he was the winner of the Turner Prize.

Richard Long lives in Bristol and continues to travel the world to make his work.

David Mach

David Mach was born in Methil, Fife, in 1956. He studied at Duncan
Jordanstone College of Art (1974-79) and at the Royal College of Art,
London (1979-82). A random look at his biography shows a life full
of activity. For example, in 1989 there are listed twelve exhibitions
or installations in ten different cities, ranging from San Francisco to
Madrid and Milton Keynes to Melbourne. This is typical of his hectic
work pattern which built up to this pitch within four years of his leaving
the Royal College, and continues unabated.

Multiple mass-produced objects, most notably magazines, newspapers
and car tyres, have been used consistently by Mach throughout his
career. He brings diverse items together in large-scale installations
with humour and social comment. His work is representational and
controversial. A work of the early 1980s, *Polaris* 1983, shown at the
Hayward Gallery in London, took the form of a submarine, but made
of used car tyres. This monumental tribute to nuclear power was set
alight by highly critical viewers who obviously failed to see its irony.

David Mach's sculpture is on the verge of being completely
overwhelming in its scale and audacity. Making classical pillars from
thousands of newspapers and magazines at the Tramway Gallery in
Glasgow in 1990 was a marathon of physical effort in which he was
helped, as in much of his work, by his wife Lesley. Papers were fanned
and stacked around existing supporting pillars in the tram sheds,
transforming them to the scale and form of columns that would support
the Acropolis. He also uses magazines to form swirling waves which
carry other objects in their turbulence. The density of these installations
is echoed in his smaller sculptures where multiple objects are used to
make the whole. Typical are the 'match head' series: portraits, similar
to Chinese and Venetian theatre masks, made from unstruck matches
glued together so that only the coloured heads show on the surface.
Sometimes these are fired to form faces of a sombre hue.

John Maine

John Maine was born in Bristol in 1942. He studied at the West of England College of Art, Bristol (1960-64) and at the Royal College of Art, London (1964-67), where he was a contemporary of Nigel Hall, Ken Draper and John Panting. A two-year fellowship at Gloucestershire College of Art followed. Travels in the Yukutan, Mexico, had an early influence on his work, and he developed the ideas generated there during the course of his fellowship at the Yorkshire Sculpture Park (1979-80), the first artist to be accorded that honour. He then lived in London, with periods of time spent in Dorset working on Portland stone and in Italy in the famous marble quarries of Carrara.

His first one-man exhibition was held at the Serpentine Gallery in London in 1972, since when he has exhibited regularly in Britain. He has also received many awards, amongst which are the Royal College of Art Drawing Prize (1967), Art Council Awards (1972, 1975 and 1977), the Mark Rothko Memorial Trust award (travel to USA and Mexico, 1979), an Elephant Trust Award for Chiswell Earthworks (1990-95) and a Henry Moore Foundation Award (1991). John Maine was elected Royal Academician in 1995.

Much of John Maine's work has been in the form of public commissions, notably the *Chiswell Earthworks* in Portland, Dorset (1986-93), the Lewisham 2000 project (from 1991) and his largest sculpture to date, the monument commemorating the completion of the Ryugasaki New Town Hokuryudai Area Development in Japan (1993). Landscape, land forms, ancient sites, structures within nature, mathematical systems, solids, surface planes and sections through forms, all have their place in John Maine's vocabulary as a sculptor. Stone, and in particular Portland stone from Dorset where he lives, is his preferred medium.

Bernard Meadows

Bernard Meadows was born in Norwich in 1915. He studied painting at Norwich School of Art (1934-37). Between 1936 and 1939, and again between 1946 and 1948, he was studio assistant to Henry Moore. He moved to London in 1937, and attended lectures at the London Institute of Education and the Courtauld Institute of Art, and painting and sculpture courses at the Royal College of Art (1938-48).

He served with the RAF (1941-46), initially in Dover and then in India, Ceylon, and in the Cocos Islands in the Indian Ocean. The world at war provided a background of insecurity, vulnerability and terror. Meadows's sculpture inevitably reflected these feelings, which have remained within his work throughout his career. On a more immediate level his keen observation of crabs in the Cocos Islands also had a lasting effect on the imagery he employs in his sculpture. Frightened birds, crab forms and vulnerable figures (protected by hard shells or armour) are constant themes in his sculpture and drawing.

Meadows taught at Chelsea School of Art, London (1948-60), and was Professor of Sculpture at the Royal College of Art (1960-80). He was appointed Professor Emeritus at the Royal College of Art in 1980. As Acting Director of the Henry Moore Foundation (1983-88) he ensured that Moore's work was enlarged in the spirit that Moore intended, and he helped to develop the generous support for artists that the Foundation continues to give today. Since 1989 he has been consultant to the Foundation. The time that Meadows spent teaching and helping artists may account for his relatively small output.

The XXVI Venice Biennale of 1952 brought his name into international prominence and his 80th Birthday Exhibition at the Yorkshire Sculpture Park in 1995 underlined his contribution to the development of sculpture in Britain.

Dhruva Mistry

Dhruva Mistry was born in Kanjari, Gujarat, India, in 1957. He studied sculpture at the Faculty of Fine Arts, MS University of Baroda (1974-79), graduating with distinction and a gold medal. He went on to gain an MA at Baroda (1979-81) and then came to Britain on a British Council Scholarship to take an MA in Sculpture at the Royal College of Art (1981-83).

From 1983 to 1996 Dhruva Mistry pursued his career as a sculptor in Britain. He has residencies at Kettle's Yard Gallery, Cambridge, with fellowships at Churchill College (1984-85) and at the Victoria and Albert Museum, London (1988). He received many awards in this thirteen-year period, including the Third Rodin Grand Prize Exhibition, Japan (1990); the Jack Goldhill award (1991); the Humanities Prize medal award in the Asian Artist Today - Fukuoka Annual VII, Fukuoka, Japan (1994); the Design President's award for the Victoria Square Sculptures, the Landscape Institute and Marsh Fountain of the Year award for Victoria Square, Birmingham (1995). Dhruva Mistry was elected Royal Academician in 1991 and was made fellow of the Royal Society of British Sculptors in 1993.

The rich imagery and narrative content of Indian art, the highly developed skills of a dedicated sculptor, working in a culture not his own, and an independence of mind which channels effort absolutely, have all contributed to Dhruva Mistry's success as a sculptor. His work ranges from huge public commissions to maquettes and wall reliefs, related in part to Hinduism and Buddhism, but also encompassing influences from the West - Egyptian and Cycladic art and European traditions of figurative sculpture. Not all his sculpture is narrative. In some work he explores the processes of making art and the inevitable intellectual debate that ensues between artist and viewer, whether implied or expressed.

David Nash

David Nash was born in Esher, Surrey, in 1945. He studied at Kingston College of Art (1963-64), Brighton College of Art (1964-67) and Chelsea School of Art (1969-70).

In 1970 he moved to Blaenau Ffestiniog where he lives and works; in that year he made his first wooden tower, since destroyed by a gale.

Nash works entirely in wood - wood that no longer has a useful life - and with living plants. Most of his museum exhibitions have been made in wood which was found in the locality of the host museums, ensuring a relevance which is unique and which neatly sidesteps the notion of being site specific in the traditional sense.

David Nash has worked regularly abroad, particularly in Japan, and enjoys considerable international acclaim, with work represented in numerous collections throughout the world.

Paul Neagu

Paul Neagu was born in Bucharest, Romania, in 1938. He studied at the Institute 'N Grigorescu' (1959-65). In 1969 he came to Britain at the invitation of Richard Demarco, and has since lived and worked in London, as a lecturer in fine art, in addition to pursuing his own career as an artist. Neagu gained British citizenship in 1977.

Paul Neagu's sculpture conveys the notion of movement through abstract form. His drawings, paintings, performances and sculpture are closely linked, in that all explore ideas that cannot be made literal in any concrete sense. They invite participation, which is demanding of the viewer's concentration, and need time as well as space to work their way into our consciousness. Star forms and geometric shapes, often made in stainless steel, with the surface worked to textures that capture and refract light, are typical of Neagu's genre.

Eilís O'Connell

Eilís O'Connell was born in Derry, Northern Ireland, in 1953. She studied at Crawford School of Art, Cork (1970-74), Massachusetts College of Art, Boston (1974-75) and again at Crawford School of Art (1975-77). Two fellowships followed: the Arts Council of Northern Ireland British School at Rome Fellowship (1983-84) and the Arts Council PS1 (New York) Fellowship (1987-88).

A distinctive sense of place that Eilís O'Connell manifests in her work may possibly have led her towards undertaking many important public commissions, mostly in urban settings. These include *Secret Station* 1991, for Cardiff Bay Art Trust at the Eastern Gateway, Cardiff, and *The Space Between* 1992, commissioned by the Milton Keynes Development Corporation. During 1994 and 1995 Eilís O'Connell worked on the design for a lifting footbridge in collaboration with Ove Arup for the River Frome at Narrow Quay in central Bristol.

O'Connell's ability to ensure a successful interaction between the object and its environment may well be rooted in her experience of the Irish landscape in which she grew up. *Secret Station*, however, referred to her experience of the British industrial landscape. Her use of steam in this piece, which was pumped out through fissures in large conical forms, a device she first used in 1990, demonstrates her response to factory chimneys and other industrial outlets.

Eilís O'Connell is particularly concerned with the notions of space within objects, spaces between them and, in turn, their spatial relationship to their place. Materials and processes are also carefully chosen, both for their appropriateness and to convey contrast or emphasis.

Ana Maria Pacheco

Ana Maria Pacheco was born in Goias, Brazil, in 1943. She studied sculpture at the University of Goias (1963-64) while at the same time studying music at the Federal University of Goias. This was followed by further studies in music and other subjects at the University of Brazil, Rio de Janiero, in 1965.

In 1966 she returned to Goias where she lectured at the School of Fine Arts and the School of Architecture at the University of Goias, and at the Institute of Art at the Federal University there until 1973. In 1973 Ana Maria Pacheco left Brazil for Britain. Here, with the support of a British Council Scholarship, she studied under the figurative sculptor Reg Butler at the Slade School of Fine Art in London until 1975. Since that time she has developed her career as a sculptor, painter and printmaker in Britain. Teaching posts have included being Head of Fine Art at Norwich School of Art, Norfolk, from 1985 to 1989.

From 1980 Ana Maria Pacheco has exhibited world-wide. In Britain significant exhibitions include the Hayward Annual (1982), and solo exhibitions in the Icon Gallery, Birmingham (1983), Camden Arts Centre, London, and the Museum of Modern Art, Oxford (1991), the Gas Hall, Birmingham Museum and Art Gallery (1994) and the City of Plymouth Museums and Art Gallery (1995). In 1997, she was Artist in Residence at The National Gallery, London.

Life is a series of journeys, and the most significant so far for Ana Maria Pacheco must have been her transition from Central Brasil to Britain. It took a long time for her, having made this drastic change, to find her way within her work. Journeying is a recurrent theme in Pacheco's work, together with mysterious narratives, melodramatic encounters, sexuality, death, power, magic and secrets.

Trupti Patel

Trupti Patel was born in Nairobi in 1957. She studied for an MA in sculpture at the Faculty of Fine Arts, MS University of Baroda, India (1974-82), and - with a British Council Scholarship - an MA in ceramic sculpture at the Royal College of Art, London (1983-85).

Solo exhibitions have been held at the Hatheesing Art Gallery, Ahmedabad (1983), the Museum of Mankind, Student Showcase, London (1986), the Hannah Peschar Sculpture Garden, Ockley (1995) and Chelmsford and Essex Museum, Chelmsford (1996). Trupti Patel's work has also been included in many group exhibitions in India, Europe and America.

Her work has always been centred on the human figure and the human condition. Early works in India were cast in plaster, and she gradually moved towards leaving her work in its original modelled state in clay which was then fired. Indian terracotta is famous for its plasticity, and for the rich red colour which absorbs and deflects Indian light to reveal form and texture to a degree unequalled by light in latitudes further north. She adds colour sparingly, usually working it into the body of the clay rather than applying it as paint to the surface.

Recurring themes in Trupti Patel's sculpture are the female form and issues surrounding the female role within the family and in society. Her upbringing in Africa and India where women hold families together with subtle strength, has endowed her with insights which have been endorsed by her subsequent exposure to changing Western values.

Patel's way of working clay is sensuous and sensitive, with here and there a contrasting twist or abrasion to shock us into awareness that not all is voluptuous and calm - there is another, contrasting world of cruelty, pain and hurt which is persistent and inevitable.

William Pye

William Pye was born in London in 1938. He studied at Wimbledon School of Art (1958-61) and at the Sculpture School of the Royal College of Art (1961-65). Pye's early and sustained interest in harnessing the largely unpredictable element of water for his sculptures was fuelled by his play and observations as a child. Most of his childhood holidays and weekends were spent near Cutmill Ponds in Surrey, a national beauty spot where the young Pye learnt to swim, playing for hours in a nearby stream. By the age of seventeen he had made his first waterfall.

His sculptures of the 1960s were abstract forms and showed Pye's preference for the traditional materials of metal and stone. Highly polished abstract and geometrical works in stainless steel of the 1970s, some of which were kinetic, became synonymous with his name. Movement, reflection and the use of light in these works led him logically to considering water as an essential part of his artistic expression. The natural world which he explores in his sculptures is interpreted through water and metal, where disarmingly simple concepts become objects of utmost sophistication and great beauty.

William Pye has undertaken many major commissions in the last fifteen years, including the well-known *Slip Stream* and *Jet Stream* water sculptures at Gatwick Airport's North Terminal (1987); a 13 by 70 metres water wall and 'portico' which formed the entrance feature to the British Pavilion at *Expo '92* in Seville (1992); *Tetra Trellis*, a tetrahedron-shaped stainless steel water sculpture at Tetra Pak UK Headquarters, Stockley Park, Middlesex (1993) and *Derby Cascade* in Market Square, Derby (1995). Numerous exhibitions of William Pye's sculptures have been held in Britain and abroad since his first solo exhibition at the Redfern Gallery, London, in 1966. He has also been the recipient of many awards, and in 1993 was elected Honorary Fellow of the Royal Institute of British Architects.

Keir Smith

Keir Smith was born in Kent in 1950. He studied fine art at the University of Newcastle upon Tyne (1969-73) and at Chelsea School of Art (1973-75). His academic interest in art of the Renaissance - painting, sculpture and architecture - is long established, but has emerged only gradually as a presence in his drawing and sculpture.

Working without an agent or dealer, Smith made his way as an artist through public commissions in the 1980s when sculpture trails and the desire for site specific sculpture prevailed. He was appointed artist in residence at Grizedale Forest, Cumbria in 1979 and made a number of publicly sited sculptures including *Towards the Open Sea* for South Hill Park in Bracknell and *Dendron* for Yorkshire Sculpture Park, both in 1983. Smith excelled in his response to such commissions, and in finding an apposite solution which referred to the history of the site and its physical nature, as with *The Iron Road* 1986 for the Forest of Dean where carved wooden railway sleepers lie in the place of a disused track, bearing references to former lives and times particular to the forest. His most recent commission is a work for Henrietta House in the West End of London. Here a sculptural frieze depicting fifteen buildings related stylistically, such as Hawksmoor's Pyramid, The Radcliffe Library and Canary Wharf, to mention only three, flows with and is relevant to the architecture. In addition to the commissions, Keir Smith has exhibited his work regularly in Britain in both solo and group shows. Particularly important was *Flint Sepulchre* at the University of Warwick in 1994.

Drawing serves Keir Smith's sculpture in an indirect way. Long periods are devoted to drawing, not to find solutions for specific sculptures, but to develop ideas. The drawings, in pencil and watercolour, have all the intensity of his sculpture and are no less a result of concentrated activity. Drawings of a different kind fill his sketchbooks and are used in the development of the sculptures.

William Tucker

William Tucker was born in Cairo in 1935, and came to England when his family returned in 1937. He studied history at Oxford University (1955-58) and sculpture at the Central and St Martin's Schools of Art, London (1959-60). Anthony Caro was teaching at St Martin's at the time, and fellow students included David Annesley, Phillip King and Isaac Witkin. Tucker was awarded the Sainsbury Scholarship in 1961 and the Peter Stuyvesant Travel Bursary in 1965. He spent two years as Gregory Fellow at Leeds University Fine Arts Department (1968-70) and represented Britain at the 1972 Venice Biennale.

William Tucker is also a writer, and in 1974 published the *Language of Sculpture* (Thames and Hudson, London) which was released in the United States in 1978 as *Early Modern Sculpture* (Oxford University Press, New York). Following the publication of the book in London he was invited to select *The Condition of Sculpture* exhibition which was held at the Hayward Gallery, London, in 1975, for which he wrote the catalogue essay. Both the book and the exhibition proved to be landmarks in the development of a certain tradition of British sculpture. Tucker moved to New York in 1978 and taught at Colombia University (1978-82) and the New York Studio School. Further fellowships followed: the Guggenheim Fellowship for Sculpture in 1981 and the National Endowment for the Arts Fellowship in 1986, the year he became an American citizen. He is currently co-chair of the Art Programme at Bard College.

Early works, made from steel or wood, were assembled and altered into abstract configurations in largely geometric form. Such compositions were later cast in plaster or concrete, and concerns for weight and gravity and the defiance of those states became important. His exhibition at the Tate Gallery in 1987 and a retrospective at the Storm King Art Centre in 1988 consolidated his reputation in America, with works being acquired by the three major New York musuems.

William Turnbull

William Turnbull was born in Dundee, Scotland, in 1922. He worked as an illustrator in Dundee (1939-41) and studied at the Slade School of Fine Art, London (1946-48). For the next two years he lived in Paris, and on returning to London he became Visiting Artist at the Central School of Arts and Crafts (1953-61). He later taught sculpture there (1964-72) and now lives and works in London.

Both painter and sculptor, Turnbull finds sources for his work in other cultures and in classicism. A Chinese mask, the gateway to a Japanese Shinto temple, a primitive artifact from the tribes of Borneo or a small Cycladic goddess might be the starting point, or indeed a final reference. Abstraction is also important to Turnbull, and the issue of the marriage between abstraction and a desire to convey information in sculpture with great economy of form and precise content. Richard Morphet, in a catalogue to the exhibition Sculpture in the Close at Jesus College, Cambridge, in 1990, sums up his work: 'Turnbull's sculptures are intensely factual and their spirit is classical. Yet in their combination of formal concentration with runic articulation and metamorphic content they have a presence which approaches the magical.'

Turnbull has exhibited widely in Britain and abroad throughout his long career. His work is in public collections throughout the world.

Glynn Williams

Glynn Williams was born in Shrewsbury in 1939. He studied at Wolverhampton College of Art (1955-61). On graduating he won a Rome Scholarship for sculpture, and until 1963 lived and worked at the British School in Rome. After his return to England he taught at a number of art colleges including Leeds. In 1976 he was appointed to run the Sculpture Department at Wimbledon School of Art, setting himself the objective of building a department with clear aims and attitudes towards sculpture.

His first solo exhibition was held at the ICA in London in 1967, since when he has exhibited regularly in Britain and occasionally abroad.

Williams is a leading sculptor of the figurative tradition. Strong and solid forms based on the human figure, sliced and altered, have recently taken over from his more naturalistic sculpture. Some have been coloured or treated in ways that render surfaces more ambiguous.

Glynn Williams is currently Professor of Sculpture at the Royal College of Art, London.

Bill Woodrow

Bill Woodrow was born in Henley-on-Thames in 1948. He studied at Winchester College of Art (1967-68), St Martin's School of Art, London (1968-71) and Chelsea School of Art, London (1971-72). On graduating he showed work in a mixed exhibition at the Museum of Modern Art in Oxford and had his first one-man show at the Whitechapel Art Gallery, London, in 1972. There followed a period of around seven years when circumstances dictated that Woodrow made very little sculpture - he taught at an Inner London comprehensive school, and then full-time on a foundation course in Essex up to 1980. He would make work occasionally, but when in 1978 he got a studio he began to make sculpture on a regular basis.

Woodrow's early sculpture was made from materials found in dumps, used car lots and scrap yards, whether he was working in Britain or abroad. Large, disused consumer goods were the vehicle for his ideas - fridges, motorcar parts, doors, bricks and armchairs altered and placed in new relationships, formed metaphors for all kinds of tales. His 'archaeological' delving into modern detritus and the consequent narrative that he makes is aptly summed up in an essay by William Feaver (*The British Show* catalogue, Art Gallery of New South Wales/The British Council, 1985): 'Ransacking the debris of present-day civilisation, Bill Woodrow fabricates comparable apparitions. His sculpture is proverbial, fabulous. Cherishing the outlandish, rejoicing in the jump cut and the shock decision, he makes dry bones live.'

Collecting as he did, and using all manner of unrelated objects in new configurations, allowed Bill Woodrow to tell stories in his sculpture, and when he began to fabricate pieces in new material in the late 1980s, the narrative element remained. Recent works, cast in bronze, still evoke their eclectic origins, and the story told is equally elusive.

Sculpture at Goodwood
British Contemporary Sculpture

Sculpture at Goodwood is the only venue in Britain where visitors can see a full range of current British Sculpture, most of which has been specially commissioned by Sculpture at Goodwood.

Twenty acres of woodland walks and glades provide an idyllic setting for forty important and innovative works by British sculptors of international reputation. Change in the display occurs monthly, with one third of the works being replaced annually as new pieces are commissioned. All sculptures are for sale.

Sculpture at Goodwood is fifty miles south of London in an area of outstanding natural beauty overlooking the Roman city of Chichester and the south coast.

Winner of the National Art Collections Fund Prize 1996

'...the finest sculpture park in the land'
Antony Thorncroft, Financial Times

'Twenty acres of Sussex park land offer a perfect setting for work by Britain's best sculptors'
Richard Cork, The Times

'Thank heavens for idyllic excellence like Goodwood'
Clare Henry, Glasgow Herald

'Confident steps into pastoral perspective'
Isabel Carlisle, The Times

The Sculpture at Goodwood Website
Bringing British sculptors and their work to an international audience

Sculpture at Goodwood's Website has been devised and implemented by Dr Christopher Thorpe. Documentation about Sculpture at Goodwood on the site is historically based on Sculpture at Goodwood books, Information and Education packs. Daily and monthly changes in the displays are recorded and placed on the site as they happen. *Sculpture of the Month* features new work. Broadcasts of Sculpture at Goodwood's study days, including film, sound recordings and still images, are made on the day of the event. Written material and images of new scuptures are published on the web site as they are installed at Goodwood and form the pages for future volumes in this series of books. Artists working at Goodwood, and manufacturing processes such as casting, fabrication, carving and construction are also being featured as the web site becomes our prime educational tool.

We are now producing Quick Time Virtual Reality film of the sculptures at Goodwood, so that when works have moved away their form and scale in relationship to the copse may be experienced by the network visitor. Some sculptures are rendered as Virtual Reality Modelling Language (VRML) models. In VRML, sculptures are observed disconnected from their surroundings and may be picked up and rotated at will by the viewer. This is akin to viewing a maquette of the sculpture and eventually we hope to work with an artist using VRML as a representation of a working model for a scupture which will be realised to full scale.

The Internet site is only part of Goodwood's cross-media scheme to promote British sculpture, to inform, to archive and to educate. Each month a leaflet on new sculpture is published which cross-refers to the Website *Sculpture of the Month* and is augmented by diskettes which run independently of an Internet connection. Sculpture at Goodwood CD ROM and DVD packages may be found on pages 142 and 143.

Digital Library, Videos and Audio Tapes

Sculpture at Goodwood has so far established a store of around 10,000 images of contemporary British sculpture and design on Digital Discs which are easy to browse and may be viewed by arrangement in the gallery. The digital library is updated constantly together with the reference library of specialist books, videos and audio tapes on the work of Sculpture at Goodwood and its artists.

Each digital disc holds around one hundred images, and the collection includes the work of: Jane Ackroyd, Edward Allington, John Atkin, Walter Bailey, Zadok Ben-David, Hamish Black, Peter Burke, Peter Burke making *Host* 1996, Anthony Caro, Lynn Chadwick, Ann Christopher, Robin Connelly, Stephen Cox, Tony Cragg, George Cutts, Richard Deacon, John Edwards, John Farnam, Laura Ford, Elisabeth Frink, Elisabeth Frink Drawings, Steve Geliot, Bruce Gernand, Andy Goldsworthy, Steven Gregory, Charles Hadcock, Nigel Hall, Nicola Hicks, Shirazeh Houshiary, Jon Isherwood, Allen Jones, Anish Kapoor, Michael Kenny, Phillip King, Bryan Kneale, Langlands and Bell, Stephen Lewis, Tim Lewis, Lilian Lijn, Kim Lim, Peter Logan, Michael Lyons, Dhruva Mistry, Cathy de Monchaux, Elizabeth de Monchaux, Nicholas Moreton, Joanna Mowbray, David Nash, Paul Neagu, Colin Nicholas, Eilís O'Connell, Rob Olins, Julian Opie, Ana Maria Pacheco, Cornelia Parker, Trupti Patel, Vong Phaophanit, Charles Poulsen, William Pye, Ronald Rae, Peter Randall-Page, Paul Roberts-Holmes, Colin Rose, Sophie Ryder, Keir Smith, Susan Stockwell, Michael Sandle, Tim Threlfell, William Tucker, William Turnbull, Roderick Tye, Richard Wentworth, Glynn Williams, Avril Wilson, Bill Woodrow.

This material will be brought together in a single Digital Versatile Disc (DVD), as the technology becomes more widely available for educational and domestic use.

Library and Commissioning Archive

As Sculpture at Goodwood commissions around twelve new sculptures a year, a considerable archive is being built as a result. Artists donate past catalogues and new publications on their work to the library, which adds to the wealth of material assembled by Wilfred and Jeannette Cass since1992 when they founded the charity.

The commissioning process is well recorded, and documentation relating to the production of sculptures and their installation at Goodwood is held on file. In the first three years this amounts to records of some thirty-three sculptures. Records contain visual as well as written and statistical information, and tell the story of how the sculpture commission came about, its realisation, installation and anything else that may occur during these processes. Some are straight-forward, others contain complex instructions for footings and installatiom, crane requirements, logistcs for moving and transporting the sculpture, conservation matters, care, recipes for treating wood and finally details relating to sales and loans.

Books and catalogues on British sculptors sit with volumes on other artists. Books on sculpture parks and gardens throughout the world reflect the many travels undertaken by the founders, when they were planning Sculpture at Goodwood, and many prove to be irreplacable as they are now out of print. There are also volumes on other art forms, garden management, historical art and reference works.

The fact that this library is being built in parallel with the digital library, CD ROMs, DVD and the Internet Site, will make Sculpture at Goodwood a centre of information on British sculpture.

Publications

Sculpture at Goodwood books are published annually and when collected form a history of commissions leading to an overview of British sculpture as seen through the works displayed at Goodwood. The first volume was published in 1995.

Whilst the sculptures in the books are illustrated in the sequence you are likely to encounter them during a walk at Sculpture at Goodwood, because of the on-going commissioning process, they are never entirely up to date. To give visitors current information, everyone receives *The Way Round*. This is a single sheet which lists sculptures on display and notes to guide visitors around the copse. Line drawings by Marion Witcomb help to identify the works listed.

The Sculpture at Goodwood video features the opening in 1994, and is a short introduction to the sculptures and intentions of the foundation.

Website developments by Dr Christopher Thorpe will result in the publication of a series of CD ROMs. The first will be a CD ROM version of this book, and will be followed by others featuring detailed accounts of individual sculptures, the making process and visual information on artists work, to place the Goodwood sculptures in context. A CD ROM version of www.sculpture.org.uk will be published from time to time.

A catalogue on Sculpture at Goodwood Drawings will be published to coincide with the launch of an international travelling exhibition of drawings, models and maquettes which are being collected as a result of commissioning sculptures. A leaflet about this exhibition is available for museum and gallery curators.

Designers

The work of young designers, most of whom are under the age of twenty-five, is an important aspect of Sculpture at Goodwood. From the time they established the foundation, Wilfred and Jeannette Cass have sought out innovative seating, signing and buildings for the grounds, as well as furniture for the gallery and office. Pieces which demonstrate an inventive use of materials and form are commissioned to show a range of design and making processes. Their display in the grounds is functional and devised to encourage others to support the work of these young people.

Items by Ben Brooks, Alison Crowther, John Greed, Thomas Heatherwick, David Harvey, James Paget, Jim Partridge, Johnny Woodford and students of Hooke Park College at Parnham in Dorset in the form of desks, seats and shelters has been commissioned over the first three years. Materials used include various native and tropical hard woods, carbon fibre, glass, perspex, green wood, metals, stones and cements. Looking to the future, we hope to add more, and to include recycled materials.

Inspirations for seating range from water (Ben Brooks) through all kinds of organic forms (Alison Crowther, James Paget, Johnny Woodford) to mathematical devices worked out with the assistance of a computer (Thomas Heatherwick). Techniques demonstrated in the collection range through casting, laminating, moulding, carving, welding and construction. Information about these works together with the addresses and telephone numbers of the designers is available for visitors in the gallery. Most pieces were illustrated in the second volume in this series, Sculpture at Goodwood 96/97.

The House and Beginnings

The house at Sculpture at Goodwood was built in 1976/77 by Charles Kearley for his fine collection of twentieth century art which he left, on his death in 1989, to Pallant House in Chichester. The house was designed in close consultation with local architects, John and Heather Lomax of Hughes, Lomax and Adutt, to the Bauhaus principles of repeated cubes and without the traditional interior finishes of plaster, skirting, architraves and cornices. Its position in the site is discreet, but with wonderful views through the woodland to Chichester and the coast.

Wilfred and Jeannette Cass bought the house from Kearley's estate in 1989, and having made minor modifications, began to move in during March 1990. Inspired by the views over distant pastures to Chichester Cathedral and the way that their own collection of sculpture was seen to advantage in the grounds, they set about creating Sculpture at Goodwood as a charitable foundation. The idea of ceasing to build a collection and devote their resources to establishing a charitable foundation to help British sculptors emerged gradually. Their research took them world-wide to many venues which show sculpture in the open air, and through their observations, critical and business-based approach, their plan for Goodwood evolved.

The foundation now commissions around twelve sculptures a year which it owns in partnership with the sculptors until the time they are sold. At the point of sale the foundation receives back its financial input and a small percentage of the selling price to cover overheads, and the money is ploughed back into new pieces. This system provides continuing support and promotion for contemporary sculpture and change in the display. A self-imposed limit of some forty pieces, placed with care in the grounds, ensures uncrowded siting and the opportunity for a unique aesthetic experience.

The Woodland Setting

In the early years much of the copse was overgrown with vines of old man's beard, and many trees had fallen in the devastating storms of 1987 and 1990. When the damaged trees and vines were cleared and spaces created for sculptures, the growth of many species of wild flowers was stimulated by light which had been excluded. Encouraged by this discovery and the success of their first season of planting, the Casses, under the guidance of landscape designer Victor Shanley, forestry engineer Peter Harland and grounds manager Martin Russell, have devised an ongoing plan of woodland renewal. Native species of broad-leaf trees replace conifers and diseased trees, adding to the diversity of stock and providing background colours that change with the seasons whilst changing visitors' experience of the sculptures.

The eastern portion of the copse has been leased at a peppercorn rent to Sculpture at Goodwood by the Duke of Richmond and Gordon, and only since 1993 has it been worked and planted. This area has provided some of the larger sweeps of lawn and long vistas over arable land to the south and north-east.

The twenty-acre site is enclosed on two sides by portions of an historic, listed flint wall which, throughout the Richmond estate, extends for seventeen miles. This was built around 1812 by French prisoners of war who were imprisoned in Portsmouth. They mined the flints locally, and some pits remain as grassed or overgrown hollows in the grounds of Sculpture at Goodwood, one of which forms the open air theatre. A small part of the wall shows the work of a master craftsman, where the napped flints are perfectly cut and mortared, whilst the effort of less skilled artisans bears a more random assembly.

Sculptures 1994-97

with page numbers for the sculptures illustrated in this volume

Edward Allington *Fallen Pediment (Piano)* 1994 [p26]

Kenneth Armitage *Richmond Oak* 1985-90 [p68]

Zadok Ben-David *Conversation Piece* 1996 [p74]

Matt Bodimeade *Force 7* 1990

Peter Burke *Host* 1996 [p84]

Sir Anthony Caro *The Tower of Discovery* 1991

Sir Anthony Caro *Goodwood Steps (Spirals)* 1994-96 [p14]

Lynn Chadwick *Stranger III* 1959 (cast 1996) [p32]

Robin Connelly *Oak Spiral* 1991

Stephen Cox *Organs of Action - speeech, evacuation, procreation, grasp, gait* 1987-88

Stephen Cox *Granite Catamarans on a Granite Wave* 1994 [p78]

Tony Cragg *Trilobites* 1989 [p66]

George Cutts *The Kiss* 1991

George Cutts *Sea Change* 1996 [p90]

Grenville Davey *Button* 1988

John Davies *Head* 1997 [p40]

Richard Deacon *When the Landmasses First Appeared* 1986 [p98]

Eva Drewett *Around Man* 1991

Eva Drewett *The Human Side of Being II* 1992

Ian Hamilton Finlay *The World Has Been Empty Since the Romans* 1985 [p30]

Laura Ford *Nature Girls* 1996

Elisabeth Frink *Horse and Rider* 1969

Elisabeth Frink *Riace Figures I, II, III, IV* 1986, 1987,1988, 1989

Bruce Gernand *Hearts-Hide* 1993

Andy Goldsworthy *Herd of Arches* 1994 [p48]

Andy Goldsworthy *A Clearing of Arches. For the Night* 1995

Steven Gregory *Bag Men* 1993

Steven Gregory *Paparazzi* 1996 [p44]

Charles Hadcock *Caesura IV* 1995 [p56]

Nigel Hall *Soglio (Goodwood)* 1994 [p96]

Shirazeh Houshiary *The Extended Shadow* 1994 [p60]

Michael Kenny *In Secrecy and Solitude* 1991-92 [p94]

Phillip King *Genghis Khan* 1963

Phillip King *Slant* 1966

Phillip King *Academy Piece* 1971

Bryan Kneale *Deemster Fish* 1996 [p54]

Langlands and Bell *Fifty Cities* 1997 [p76]

Kim Lim *Spiral II* 1983

Peter Logan *Duet for Two Flutes* 1991

Richard Long *Six Stone Circles* 1981 [p70]

Michael Lyons *Amphitrite* 1993

David Mach *The Garden Urn* 1996 [p52]

David Mach *The Wild Bunch!* 1996 [p22]

John Maine *Enclosure* 1995 [p18]

Bernard Meadows *Large Seated Armed Figure* 1963 [p46]

Dhruva Mistry *The Object* 1995-97 [p34]

David Nash *Charred Column* 1993

David Nash *Two Together* 1994 [p86]

David Nash *Mosaic Eggs* 1995 [p36]

Paul Neagu *Triple Star Head* 1987-93 [p50]

Paul Neagu *Unnamed (Eschaton)* 1997 [p92]

Eilis O'Connell *Space Emptied Out* 1994 [p88]

Ana Maria Pacheco *Requiem* 1986-95 [p16]

Trupti Patel *Stay* 1995 [p28]

Vong Phaophanit *Azure Neon Body* 1994-95

William Pye *Vessel III* 1995 [p64]

Peter Randall-Page *Ways to Wrap a Stone I* 1990

Peter Randall-Page *Ways to Wrap a Stone II* 1990

Peter Randall-Page *Beneath the Skin* 1991

Peter Randall-Page *Secret Life I & IV* 1994

Colin Rose *Breeze* 1991

Colin Rose *Night and Day* 1992

Sophie Ryder *The Boxing Hares* 1988

Michael Sandle *A Mighty Blow for Freedom: Fuck the Media* 1988

Keir Smith *Stefano* 1997 [p38]

William Tucker *Frenhofer* 1997 [p80]

William Turnbull *Large Spade Venus* 1986

William Turnbull *Gate* 1972 [p72]

Glynn Williams *Portrait with Flowers* 1990-91

Glynn Williams *Gateway of Hands* 1992 [p20]

Avril Wilson *A Leaf with Halo* 1991

Bill Woodrow *Endeavour: Cannon Dredged from the First Wreck of the Ship of Fools* 1994 [p62]

Bill Woodrow *Sitting on History I* 1990-95 [p82]

Ackowledgements

Jane Allison

Robert Allison

Ian Barker

Roger Bamber

Pam Barnett

David Barrie

Rob Bevan

Mary-Rose Beaumont

Erica Bolton

Sir Alan Bowness

Ivor Braka

Sir Anthony Caro

Tim Carrigan

Mark & Dana Cass

Eric & Jean Cass

Helen Codd

David Cohen

Sir Terence Conran

Gill Coope

Maria de Corral

Henry-Claude Cousseau

Bronny Cunningham

John Dewey

Craig Downie

Nigel Draffan

Peter Eade

Jason Edwards

Nicholas Elam

Biddy Elkins

Hilary Escolme

Nicholas Fisk

Angela Flowers

Julia Fogg

Sir Norman Foster

Martin Friedman

Christopher Fry

Rudi Fuchs

David Gordon

David Gronow

Geraldine Hamilton

Kevin Hankey

Peter Harland

Jurgen Harten

Gill Hedley

Angus & Anne Hewat

Ros Hitchens

Robert Hopper

Michael Hue-Williams

David Hurren

Image Bank

Barbara Jensen

Annely Juda

Janet Kahn

Jo Kelly

David Laker

Judy Lane

Jill & Stuart Le Fevre

Sir Tom Lighton

Tim Llewellyn

Nicholas Logsdail

Annette Lovell

Prof Norbert Lynton

Elizabeth McCrae

Bill Malaclei

Earl of March

Tim Marlow

Brian Miles

Peter Mimpress

Victoria Miro

Richard E Mitchell

David Mitchinson

Amanda Moses

Peter Murray

Gerry Nutbeem

William Packer

Michael Peat

Ivan Pope

Jane Quinn

Caroline Read

Duke of Richmond

Bryan Robertson

Martin Russell

Liz Sarginson

Jo Seal

David Sekers

Nicholas Serota

Victor Shanley

Phil Stroud

Eleanor Thomas

Betty Thomson

Peter & Jean Thorpe

Leslie Waddington

Margaret Weld

Julia Whyard

Rob Widdows

Bill Witcomb

Jonathan Witcomb

Marion Witcomb

Mark Wrey

Tim Wright

Gillian Young

Index

Copyright © 1997
Sculpture at Goodwood

Texts
Ann Elliott

Editing
Angela Dyer

Design
Mervyn Kurlansky
Marianne Moller
Dr Christopher Thorpe

Photography
Frank Naylor

Printing
Crown Colourprint Limited

ISBN
0 9525233 3 7

Sculpture at Goodwood
Goodwood, West Sussex PO18 0QP
Telephone +44 (0)1243 538449
Fax +44 (0)1243 531853
Directions +44 (0)1243 771114
e-mail w@sculpture.org.uk
Internet www.sculpture.org.uk
reg charity no. 1015088

Open March-November
Thursday, Friday, Saturday 10.30 am - 4.30 pm